WHAT ARE YOU LIVING FOR?

John Sutherland Bonnell

WHAT ARE YOU LIVING FOR

ABINGDON PRESS
New York ● *Nashville*

WHAT ARE YOU LIVING FOR?

Copyright MCML by Pierce & Smith

Library of Congress Catalog Card Number: 50-5254

B

PRINTED AND BOUND AT NASHVILLE,
TENNESSEE, UNITED STATES OF AMERICA

To

The Memory of

MY MOTHER

CATHERINE CAMERON BONNELL

Foreword

⚬⚬⚬

THESE SERMONS deal with problems personal and social of our day. Many of them are relevant to the evangelistic emphasis which concerns us all so vitally. It is my hope that they may indicate, even though it be all too inadequately, how the challenge of the Christian evangel may be presented to congregations of modern-day persons.

They have grown out of my preaching from the pulpit of the Fifth Avenue Presbyterian Church, New York, during the past two years. Many of them have been presented, with some modifications, on the radio program "National Vespers." "The Faith That Transforms" and "I Believe in the Holy Catholic Church" have appeared in the *Christian Century Pulpit*. "Making Your Life Significant" has appeared in the *Christian World Pulpit*. "You Are the Hope of the World" has appeared under another title in the *Official Bulletin* of the Board of Christian Education of the Presbyterian Church, U. S. A.

This is the first volume of sermons I have published in thirteen years, and it is offered in response to repeated requests from the radio audience as well as the friendly urging of my loyal congregation.

JOHN SUTHERLAND BONNELL

Contents

❧

INVITATION TO ADVENTURE

FROM DOUBT INTO FAITH

COURAGE TO OVERCOME

9

INVITATION TO ADVENTURE

The Master Passes By

And after these things he went forth, and saw a publican, named Levi, sitting at the receipt of custom: and he said unto him, Follow me. And he left all, rose up, and followed him.—LUKE 5:27-28

IT IS AN incontrovertible fact that a single happening may permanently change the tenor of a human life. John Keats, at the age of eighteen, was handed by a school friend a copy of Spenser's "Faerie Queene." No sooner had he begun to read the poem than the soul of the youth was kindled with heavenly inspiration. Instantly he knew that he was destined to be a poet.

John Masefield, a roving, seafaring lad of twenty-two, happened upon a copy of one of Chaucer's poems. He read it with absorbing interest. That poem became the means of introducing him into what he calls: "A glad new world of thought in fellowship with Shakespeare, Milton, Shelley, and Keats."

Jenny Lind, a struggling young music student of Stockholm, one day discovered that she had a glorious voice. Her entire outlook on life was immediately changed. This is how she describes the experience: "I got up that morning one creature; I went to bed another creature. I had found my power."

It is doubtful if any of these determinative experiences ever happens like a bolt from the blue. In all these instances there was a period of preparation or "incubation," as the

13

psychologists would call it. This is true, whether it be a
poet awakening suddenly to a knowledge of his powers or
a soul transformed by the spirit of God.

La Cordaire, the French scientist, wrote: "I was unbelieving in the evening and on the morrow I was a Christian,
certain with an invincible certainty." The life of Augustine
also illustrates this fact. Tortured by doubts and fears, he
lay on the grass in his garden at Milan, muttering: "O Lord,
how long? Tomorrow and tomorrow and tomorrow."
Then, from within his own soul came a voice that said:
"Take up and read." Opening the Bible that lay beside him,
he read a flaming page from the pen of Paul, and his eye
lighted upon several verses that gripped his mind and spirit:
"Let us walk honestly, as in the day; not in rioting and
drunkenness, not in chambering and wantonness, not in
strife and envying. But put ye on the Lord Jesus Christ, and
make not provision for the flesh, to fulfil the lusts thereof."

This is how he speaks of this incident: "I opened the
book and read in silence the chapter on which my eye first
fell. I cared to read no further, nor was there any need of
it, since at once with the ending of the verse the light of
security was passed into my heart, and all the gloom of hesitation fled away." While it is true that Christ broke upon
these souls with all the glory of the sunrise, there were earlier
tokens of the coming of the dawn.

Luke in his Gospel says: "And after these things he went
forth, and saw a publican, named Levi, sitting at the receipt
of custom: and he said unto him, Follow me. And he left
all, rose up, and followed him." There is good reason to believe that this was not the first meeting that Levi or Matthew, as he is sometimes called, had had with our Lord. For
some weeks the Master had been preaching in the vicinity of
Capernaum. Doubtless Matthew had listened to his mes-
sages. It may well be that standing on the fringe of the
crowd, on more than one occasion, he had heard the Lord.
These publicans were so unpopular with the multitude that

Levi, being one of them, dared not enter the midst of the throng. As he listened, the unforgettable words of our Lord floated over the heads of the people and found lodgment in his heart. "Whosoever will come after me, let him deny himself, and take up his cross, and follow me. . . . For what shall it profit a man, if he gain the whole world, and lose his own soul? Or what shall a man give in exchange for his soul?" As Matthew turned and made his way back to the custom house, he walked with leaden feet and a heavy heart. As he opened the ledgers again, on every page, burning like letters of fire, were these words: "What shall it profit a man, if he gain the whole world and lose his own soul?"

In his conscience a voice sounded unceasingly: "What is the profit, Matthew? What is the profit? And don't forget the loss."

This man, Levi, had sold himself to the Romans as a tax collector. In our day he would be called a Quisling, a hireling of the occupying forces. He had been despised so long by his fellow countrymen that he had come at last to despise himself. Now he began to loathe the dishonesty and extortion of his office. Yet it was by these unjust exactions that he had made himself the richest man in Capernaum.

Haunting him by night and by day, sounding down all the corridors of his soul, were the Master's words: "Whosoever will come after me, let him deny himself, and take up his cross, and follow me." Matthew bowed his head upon his clenched fists and said: "O God, if I had the courage to do it!" In such a moment he became aware of a shadow that had fallen across the table, and, looking up, he found himself gazing into the face of the Master. The searching, yet tender, eyes of Jesus explored his soul, reading the story of bitter anguish and inner conflict.

For the first time since Matthew had become a publican he looked into human eyes not filled with condemnation and hate. In amazement he saw in the face of Jesus only understanding, sympathy, and love. For a moment that seemed like an eternity Jesus continued to look into Matthew's heart, and, then, laying his hand gently on the publican's shoulder, he said: "Matthew, follow me." Without a word the publican rose and left all and followed him. Matthew, who for many years had lived only for money, now became a disciple of him who had nowhere to lay his head. I think that it was Jesus who changed the name of Levi to that of Matthew, for Matthew means "given of God."

The sensational news of this conversion spread swiftly through Capernaum. "Have you heard who is the latest disciple of the Galilean? Levi."

"Not that accursed publican?"

"Yes, the very man."

"What on earth good can that scoundrel do?"

What good can he do? Before Jesus had finished with him, he was so inspired by his great love for the Master, that he raised a memorial to his name that will be remembered through all generations when the glory of Capernaum shall have crumbled into dust and its very site by the shores of the sea of Galilee will have been forgotten of man. A memorial? What memorial? It is known as the Gospel According to St. Matthew. Alexander Whyte had the right of it. He said that Matthew did not leave everything behind him that day when he quit the custom house; he took along his pen.

The secret of Jesus' success with Matthew lay in the fact that, while his townspeople judged the publican by externals, Jesus looked deep into his heart. Remember how our Lord said: "Judge not according to the appearance"? It would seem that Paul learned well the ways of the Master, for he writes: "Estimate no man by what is external."

Yet isn't this the way we form most of our judgments of people? We see only the outside: the clothes, the expression, the voice, the manner. We say: "He is cold, hard, unresponsive, incorrigible, really bad." Sometimes even the final judgment we pass upon people is based wholly on externals.

A little time ago I discussed with a church group the question: "How can one judge any other way than by externals? How can one see beneath them?" At the moment I wasn't certain as to the answer to that question. Now I am confident that I have it. We learn the answer as we watch Jesus in his dealings with men and women, and especially with Matthew. The answer is this: We see beneath the externals of a human life when we look at it with the eyes of love. We must learn to love people more—unpleasant people, gruff and rude people, hard-looking and cold people. Love enables us to detect a great tenderness beneath the rough exterior, and a true humanity under the cover of callous indifference. Love is the secret. The world is hungry for love. People are perishing for lack of love. Christ came to kindle love in our hearts for all men, and where love is there God is also.

"Why do you travel all the way across the city of Chicago to attend Mr. Moody's Sunday school?" a young lad with a not-too-prepossessing appearance was asked. He hesitated a moment, and then replied: "Because they love a fellow over there."

It was the love of Christ shining forth in the great heart of Dwight L. Moody which brought fifteen hundred street urchins together every Sunday, and ultimately made some of them leaders of church and community life, and one of them postmaster of Chicago and commander-in-chief of the Grand Army of the Republic.

"Follow me," said Jesus to Matthew. He presented the same challenge to Andrew and Peter, James and John, Nathanael and Philip, and all others that make up the glorious company of the Apostles.

The call of Christ transformed ordinary men into spiritual giants. After their call there ensued a long period of training and discipline. They walked and talked with the Master and caught something of his spirit. When we have once answered the call of Christ, let us always remember that such a response is only the beginning of the Christian life. Christian discipleship is not a temporary, emotional experience. There must be long years of training in the school of Christ. Said the great Apostle, Paul: "Grow in grace and in the knowledge of our Lord and Saviour, Jesus Christ."

When anyone answers the call of Christ his character undergoes a transformation. The prophet Hosea describes an experience of religious awakening: "Break up your fallow ground: for it is time to seek the Lord, till he come and rain righteousness upon you." There are tremendous spiritual potentialities in all of us as there were in Matthew, but the soil must be broken up and cultivated.

Dr. F. B. Meyer of London told me of an English land-owner who took him out to see a field that he had acquired only a year earlier. When he purchased the property the soil was damp, coarse, and uncultivated. It produced only thistles. The new owner drained and plowed the field. To his amazement it brought forth a rich crop of clover. The long-buried seed had remained starved and dormant until cultivation permitted sunshine to enter the soil and quicken the seed into life.

Human lives are just like that field. Break up the fallow ground—the hard unproductive ground. Give your soul a chance for self-expression. It will surprise you what a harvest you will produce to the glory of God and the blessing of yourself and others.

John Masefield, in the poem *The Everlasting Mercy*, tells of the conversion of Saul Kane, the coarsened, hardened, liquor-soddened man. With liberated soul Kane looked out across the field and saw a plowman at the task of God. Instantly he realized that Christ was plowing in his heart.

> Through rest-harrow and bitter roots,
> Through all my bad life's rotten fruits.

Then he sees the sea gulls soaring after the plowman, and in ecstasy he cries:

O Christ who holds the open gate,
O Christ who drives the furrow straight,
O Christ, the plough, O Christ the laughter
Of holy white birds flying after.[1]

"Break up your fallow ground: for it is time to seek the Lord." Rise up now and follow Christ. I confront you today, not with a program, but with a Person; not with a body of dogma to be received, but with a life to be lived; not with a creed, but with the inescapable Christ.

To you today, as to Matthew in the long ago by the blue waters of Galilee, Christ is saying: "Follow me."

[1] Copyright 1911 by John Masefield. Used by permission of the Macmillan Co., publishers.

The Miracle of Changed Men

Therefore, if any man be in Christ, he is a new creature: old things are passed away; behold all things are become new. —II Cor. 5:17

ANY VISITOR to the ruins of the Colosseum in Rome who uses his imagination can readily conceive the effect upon the population when they witnessed Christian martyrdom. Tertullian, writing near the close of the second century, describes the behavior of the Roman populace as they beheld the death of Christians. He speaks of the hideous shouting and clamor of the mob, their insatiable thirst for blood, the uneasiness that gripped the spectators after they watched Christian men, women, and children heroically die for their faith. On occasions the populace left the arena subdued by the tranquillity and courage of those who had unflinchingly laid down their lives out of love for their crucified but risen Master. Tertullian adds: "No man would be willing to die unless he knew he had the truth." The blood of the martyrs was indeed the seed from which new Christians sprang.

It was not otherwise with the death of Stephen, the first Christian martyr. Saul of Tarsus, a young Pharisee who had come to Jerusalem for post-graduate studies at the feet of the eminent scholar, Gamaliel, had watched Stephen die. Saul was one of the leaders of the mob that killed him. The witnesses laid down their clothes at his feet so that they might better hurl the stones which would silence forever the eloquent young Christian Stephen. With implacable hate in his face, Saul of Tarsus watched while the dying martyr lifted himself up and, with his last expiring breath, cried: "Lord, lay not this sin to their charge." When the persecutor described the happening in later years, with tears streaming down his face he added: "And when he had said this, he fell asleep."

From the day that he witnessed Stephen's martyrdom Saul did not know a moment of peace. His hatred of the crucified Galilean and his followers became intensified. Yet always he was gravely uneasy lest he should be found fighting against God. He illustrated what the psychologists mean by a divided self. He could cry with Faust: "Two souls, alas, dwell in my breast apart." Yet instead of making his peace with God, he flung himself more furiously upon the Christians.

Goethe once said: "The man who acts never has a conscience; no one has any conscience but the man who thinks." The German philosopher might have added that some people engage in feverish activity to keep themselves from thinking. It was so with Saul of Tarsus. He had himself made public prosecutor of the Christians. Shortly thereafter he secured the necessary official documents and set out for Damascus "breathing threatenings and slaughter against the disciples of the Lord." It was his plan to bring them bound to Jerusalem, where they would stand trial. For his own peace of mind, Saul of Tarsus chose the wrong mission.

The distance from Jerusalem to Damascus is 160 miles. Much of it lay across a desert. Saul had plenty of time for thought. Mentally he began to review the events of the past months—the happiness of Christian homes whose sanctuary he had violated; the blameless lives of these followers of Christ, and always the face of Stephen rising up before him as he said: "Lord, lay not this sin to their charge."

The heart of the young Pharisee was filled with tumultuous emotions as he drew near Damascus. Soon the fertile plain lay in full view, with its orchards and green fields, and the rivers Abana and Pharpar winding through it like silver threads. The brilliant noonday sun was reflected from the white domes of the city.

He urged the cavalcade on. His prey was almost in sight. He would soon drown these distressing thoughts in vigorous action. But in that instant a marvelous thing happened. He found himself prostrate on the ground, dazzled by a blinding light. Deep within him a voice was sounding: "Saul, Saul, why persecutest thou me?" The question was not: "Why do you persecute the Christian Church?" but "Why persecutest thou me?" for every blow that was struck against the cause of Christ was a blow struck at the Church's King and Head.

"Who art thou, Lord?" came the faltering question, and the reply "I am Jesus whom thou persecutest: it is hard for thee to kick against the pricks."

Now came the moment of unconditional surrender. The lips of the penitent persecutor uttered these words: "Lord, what wilt thou have me to do?" From that moment he was a Christ-mastered man. The truth of the Resurrection broke upon him with compelling power. He was certain that it was the risen Christ who met him that day on the road to Damascus.

Years later, writing to one of the churches that he had founded, Paul said: "If any man be in Christ, he is a new creation." His own life illustrated these words; he had been re-created. Here is a spiritual miracle that defies naturalistic explanation. The pitiless persecutor becomes the greatest of the Apostles. The man who had made it his business to hunt down, to imprison, to torture, and to kill Christians is now the fearless advocate of the gospel which he had blasphemed. The hand that had been dyed in the blood of Christian martyrs takes up a pen and writes: "Be ye kind one to another, tenderhearted, forgiving one another, even as God for Christ's sake has forgiven you."

What kind of a Master did you find him, Paul? How did you fare on your Christian pilgrimage? You had a hard, cruel road. Beaten within an inch of your life at Philippi, stoned and left for dead at Lystra, torn almost limb from limb by the maddened mob at Jerusalem, shipwrecked in the Mediterranean, now you are seated in a lonely cell in Nero's prison. Outside the door you can hear the measured tread of the Roman sentry. You know that before many days will have passed you will hear the rasping of bolts and the light of a torch will be reflected from the blade of a naked sword. It has been a hard road for you, Paul, and this is a dreadful end.

Look at the man in his cell. He is seated writing his last will and testament. Let us lean over his shoulder and see what he has written. "The drops of my sacrifice are falling fast. My time to go has come. I have fought a good fight. I have finished my course. I have kept the faith. Henceforth there is laid up for me a crown of righteousness which the Lord, the righteous judge, shall give me at that day."

A crown of righteousness! Not a crown of gold, for "uneasy lies the head" that wears that crown. So in a blaze of triumph ends the earthly career of the Apostle Paul. He and all his fellow Christians knew that his execution but opened a door for him into the presence of the Master whom he had loved and served so well.

"If any man be in Christ, he is a new creation: old things are passed away; behold, all things are become new." Here is the answer to our most baffling problem, that of creating in the hearts of men the will to understanding and peace. Man has never yet learned to live happily and co-operatively with his fellows. That is why so many friendships are shattered, so many marriages fail, so many personality clashes occur, so much bitterness exists between management and labor and between nations and races. So we falter and fumble in our effort to establish an international organization for the maintenance of peace. Our failure is a human failure.

We need a power that can enter into human hearts and transform them; that can accomplish the miracle of a new creation.

Every pastor-counselor who deals with the deepest needs of men and women has seen this wondrous thing happen: the transformation of human personalities. How is this consummation achieved? Not by force of will power, but by the "expulsive power of a new affection."

Dr. Thomas Chalmers of Scotland has given us a clue to the mystery. One day as he was riding beside the stage driver, he watched him wielding his whip with great dexterity. It flicked the legs of the off-leader. The steed, which had become restive for a moment, quieted down.

"Why did you do that?" Dr. Chalmers asked.

The driver answered: "Yonder is a white stone. Every time we pass it, this off-leader shies. I touched him with the whip to divert his attention."

Dr. Chalmers became lost in thought. When he went back to his study, he penned one of the famous sermons of history entitled "The Expulsive Power of a New Affection."

What is the new affection of which Dr. Chalmers preached? It is the affection that transformed the heart of Saul of Tarsus, expelling the emotions of resentment and hate, filling him with the spirit of love. This is a repeatable miracle. It is happening day by day.

In Stony Mountain Penitentiary, Canada, I once had an unforgettable experience. I had been conducting a mission there. One day a fair-haired fine-looking youth of about nineteen years of age walked into the room where, by special permission, I was seeing the convicts in privacy. He told me the unhappy story of the beginning of a criminal career. One of his companions had suggested a hold-up, and entrusted the loaded gun to him. Something went wrong as they tried to rob a drugstore. In panic he fired the gun and wounded the man behind the counter. Then followed days and nights of terror as he waited for the inevitable visit of the police. One evening when he was in his bedroom he heard the doorbell ringing. When his father answered the door, two men walked in saying: "We have a warrant for the arrest of your son." Leaning over the stairway, the youth heard his father say: "Gentlemen, I am very sorry, but someone has blundered. It can't be my boy you are after. Jack is a wonderfully fine fellow. I am sure he can explain everything." One of the detectives answered: "Well, we can have the explanation later. All we are interested in now is to get our hands on him." The convict looked at me and said: "I knew the jig was up, so I walked down the stairs. My father turned to me and said: 'Jack, tell the officers that there is a mistake. I am sure you haven't done anything wrong.' I had to say to one of the best fathers that God ever gave to a boy: 'I am sorry, father, but they are right. There is no mistake. I was in on that robbery.'"

The young convict sobbed as he continued: "My father's face went white as death. He placed his hand on my shoulder, and said: 'Son, no matter what trouble you are in, I believe in you, and will stand by you always.' I shall never forget the look on my father's face," the youth said. "I knew that I had broken his heart. All this came back to me as I listened to you speak. When you talked about the Cross of Christ, I thought of how my father suffered for me. I want to make a new beginning, and give my life to Christ, and I want to do it now."

In that moment came the miracle of the New Creation. This young man has long since left the penitentiary, and is carrying on with notable credit in the business and church life of his native city.

This is not an isolated and unrepeatable incident. It is happening again and again. Listen to the words of Underwood in his dispassionate psychological study of conversion: "The most remarkable fruit of conversion is seen in the manner in which it has brought about complete and permanent deliverance from every known sin. Indisputable evidence on this point is so abundant that we are embarrassed with a wealth of riches."

The expulsive power of the love of Christ works that transformation, and enables men and women to win a resounding victory where before they had met only humiliating defeat. It can do that for you. It can do it for you now.

Seeing God Face to Face

*And Jacob called the name of the place Peniel:
for I have seen God face to face, and my life is preserved.* —Gen. 32:30

ON ONE occasion Alfred Lord Tennyson asked his friend,
the English artist Watts, to explain what he considered to be
the chief duty of a portrait painter. Watts replied in effect
that his task was not merely to produce a likeness of his subject, but to reveal something of his character. Tennyson
thereupon embodied the artist's answer in "The Idylls of the
King":

> As when a painter, poring on a face,
> Divinely, thro' all hindrance finds the man
> Behind it, and so paints him that his face,
> The shape and color of a mind and life,
> Lives for his children . . .

Just as a portrait painter, at his best, shows the real man,
so the authors of the historical books of the Old Testament find the man behind the outer façade of personality and
reveal him to us. If he has defects of character, no attempt
is made to gloss them over. If he is noble, his nobility shines
forth undimmed.

Oliver Cromwell was seated, on one occasion, for a portrait, when he observed the efforts of the artist to eliminate
a slight disfiguration on his face. The Lord Protector of
England thundered, "Paint me wart and all!"

That is exactly what the biographers of the Old and the

27

New Testament have done. They portrayed the weakness as well as the strength of the characters they were reporting.

It would be difficult to find a more fitting illustration of what we have been thinking than is afforded by the life of Jacob. He had plenty of defects, and they were not over-looked. He was shrewd, calculating, industrious, with a warped character. He had a flair for hard bargaining, and found it easy to cut corners. He did not hew to the line in truthfulness and honesty.

In his defense it must be admitted that he had a very bad start. His home environment was a serious handicap. I have often wondered why the Church of England in its marriage service employed these words: "As Isaac and Rebecca lived faithfully together, so these persons may surely perform and keep the vow and covenant betwixt them made." It would in truth have been better if in the marriage service a prayer had been inserted to the effect that the newly-married couple might not keep their vows after the fashion of Jacob and Rebecca. In their case we see that which always produces tragic consequences—a house divided against itself. The father and the elder son were on one side; the mother and the younger on the other. The wife took advantage of her husband's blindness to cheat the elder son out of the blessing to which he was entitled, and trained her younger son in falsehood and deception. Despite the beautiful romance with which Isaac and Rebecca's love story begins, it ends in sordidness.

Professor George Adam Smith, one of the ablest of Old Testament scholars, says: "The fear of God was not present; because with the romance there was no religion, and with the giving of one heart to the other there was no surrender of both to God." May not this be the reason why so many marriages are failing in America today? These considerations should produce solemn reflections. We are reminded of the almost creative influence which parents exercise on the lives of their children. There are exceptions, of course, but in the main our children will carry with them through life the impact and impressions of their home life and of the character of their parents. Whatever else we bequeath to our children, let us not forget to give to them a sense of God and his government of life. Not all mothers have been a blessing to their children. Much of the falseness of Jacob's mother was stamped on his character. Deceitfulness flowed in his veins.

Now we see him fleeing to far-off Padanaram to his mother's brother to escape the wrath of Esau, his own brother, whom he had shamefully betrayed.

Laban, the uncle, gives Jacob a warm and hearty welcome, befitting a nephew, but Laban was not long in demonstrating that he was his sister's brother.

Treachery seemed to run in that family. Laban's relations with his nephew Jacob were characterized throughout by duplicity. Jacob was cheated out of his wages, out of his wife, out of all solemn obligations and promises that Laban had made to him. But it was not long until Jacob demonstrated that he too was no novice when it came to double-dealing. He proceeded to cheat his uncle out of his cattle. Then, as if to round out the picture nicely, Rachel, Laban's daughter, stole her father's household gods.

Jacob's sojourn with Laban is one pitiful chapter of fraud. There is but one gleam of light in it all—Jacob's love for Rachel. It is described in these graphic and moving words: "Jacob served seven years for Rachel and they seemed to him but a few days for the love he had to her."

But the climax, the supreme moment, in the life of this young man with the twisted character came when he turned back to Canaan from Padanaram. The crisis was reached the night before he was to meet Esau.

A great fear clutched at the heart of Jacob, for, turning homeward, he had to face again the brother whom he had defrauded. Always resourceful, however, he chose the finest and whitest of his cattle and of his sheep and of his oxen and of his camels, and he sent them forward in bands to his brother as a present to appease his bitter, flaming wrath. But the scouts brought back the disturbing word that Esau scarcely glanced at the lowing milk-white kine, but, instead, buckled on his armor and was advancing with four hundred men.

This, I say, was the supreme moment of Jacob's life— the moment for which all the rest was but a prelude.

As night begins to fall, Jacob rests beside the brook Jabbok, having sent the children and the women away to a place of safety. He waits there in the darkness alone with God.

It is always an eventful hour in the life of any man when he is alone with God; when he takes his life, and looking back over it, asks himself: "Exactly what have I made of it all?"

First of all, Jacob realized that he had become rich and successful. He had left home a penniless fugitive, a wanderer on the face of the earth, his only possessions the clothing he wore, and the little bundle his mother had thrust under his arm, containing bread and dates and oil for his journey. By dint of shrewdness and hard work and scheming he had become one of the richest men in all Palestine. He had a great retinue of servants and of flocks and of herds. But somehow he was dissatisfied that night, and he was afraid. His past had caught up with him, and God help any of us in the moment when the past catches up with us and we have no defense.

There in the loneliness and darkness of the night with the sound of the rushing brook in his ears, and only God for his companion, he looked steadfastly at his life, and, somehow, many of those things for which he had struggled and labored and cheated now seemed paltry and insignificant. Jacob remembered that he had left God out of his reckoning and that he had forgotten to lay up "treasures in heaven, where neither moth nor rust doth corrupt, and where thieves do not break through and steal."

Once before he had been alone with God in the mountains

near Bethel, but it made little change in his life. After his fashion, he tried to drive a hard bargain even with God. This is the prayer he made: "If God will be with me, and will keep me in this way that I go, and will give me bread to eat, and raiment to put on, so that I come again to my father's house in peace; then shall the Lord be my God." If God will supply all my wants and grant me prosperity and preserve me from every danger, then he will be my God!

But there was no bargaining that lonely night by the brook Jabbok. Instead he began that strange contest in the darkness. I don't think Jacob ever really understood what happened to him that night. The Scripture says: "And Jacob was left alone, and there wrestled a man with him until the breaking of the day."

As Jacob wrestled, at times that mystic wrestler in the darkness seemed to be his brother, Esau, seeking vengeance; at the next moment it was his better self wrestling with the ignoble self and seeking to overthrow it; and then it was God with whom he was grappling. Whoever that Presence was, the crafty, scheming Jacob had met his match. Here was strength he could not overcome; here was skill he could not master. And now, exhausted, he clings, and there is not a word about food and raiment. There is not a word about prosperity and protection. One cry only he utters: "I will not let thee go except thou bless me." Jacob clinging was mightier than Jacob wrestling.

Jacob learned that night what all of us must understand: that surrender to God is the condition of spiritual effectiveness and power. Jacob received the blessing and a new name. "Thy name shall be called no more Jacob, the Supplanter, the Deceiver, but Israel: for as a prince hast thou power with God and with men, and hast prevailed. . . . And he blessed him there."

"And Jacob called the name of the place Peniel: for I have seen God face to face . . ."

Our chief purpose in looking at this ancient story is not

for its dramatic quality, but to see what lessons it may teach us in the living present. It is not an exaggeration to say that the experience of Jacob more than three thousand years ago is paralleled in the lives of multitudes today.

Indeed, the unregenerate Jacob, the overly-ambitious, the hard-driving seeker of success has his prototype in a large segment of American civilization. We worship success. We have made a god of it, and before its shrine tens of thousands bow in homage. Our supreme objective is to surpass all others by our achievements.

This nation is full of men and women who are hurling themselves into life with such reckless abandon that they are wringing themselves physically and spiritually dry. Their eyes are fastened on the glittering prize of material success. At last with one supreme effort it is in their grasp. They have reached the goal, only to find that the badge of their success is a stomach ulcer or a thrombosis.

There is something about material success that but for the grace of God destroys spirituality in the human heart, because such success brings power, and power deludes its possessor into the belief that he is greater than God. When a man gets that idea into his head, he is dangerous to himself and to everybody else.

A few months ago I sat in the study of a well-known Presbyterian minister. He introduced me to a young alert-looking businessman. After the young man had gone, the minister's face clouded, and he said: "That is one of the ablest young men I have in my church. He is going far and he is getting there fast, but I am afraid for him."

I asked: "Why are you afraid?"

He replied: "He has a wife and two dear little children. In my experience in the ministry I have seen many men like him go to pieces in the very moment of achieving success. Prosperity and success are the twin rocks on which many a happy home and a useful life have been wrecked.

It is hard," the minister concluded, "for many of our American men to stand success and prosperity."

If you wish to verify the truth of this minister's words, just look at the leadership in the business and professional life of many of our great American cities. In many cases they are men who once had a vital religious experience and a happy home life. Today they have neither, and their children, faced with a divided allegiance, are bewildered and frustrated.

It is too high a price to pay for material success. It is not success in any true understanding of the word. What consummate folly for any man, no matter how great his business, professional, or political achievements, to think that he no longer needs God or that he can dispense with the Ten Commandments, or that he no longer owes an obligation to Christ's Church or his Kingdom!

Strut as he will for his brief day on life's stage, the time will come when he will find himself in a darkened room, with the shades drawn, and everyone walking on tiptoe and conversing in whispers. All his prestige and power will vanish with his last expiring breath, and his soul, stripped of the accumulations of a lifetime, will stand naked and alone before its Maker, for, "We brought nothing into this world, and it is certain we shall carry nothing out." The scales of divine justice will sway, and through all the corridors of eternity will be heard the decree: "Weighed in the balances and found wanting." The poor little man who thought he was bigger than God!

But who is there of us today that is not found wanting? What have you made of life? What have you made of yourself? What have you contributed to the world and to your fellow men? Is the world one whit happier and better because you passed this way? What have you accumulated of the true riches that death cannot destroy?

God grant us the wisdom of Jacob, who surrendered his life to the One who alone could make him great.

The Road to Certainty

*One thing I know, that, whereas I was blind,
now I see.* —JOHN 9:25

ONE OF THE dramatic moments in the history of modern science occurred in the year 1919, one year after the close of the First World War. Two scientific expeditions set forth from Britain, one to Brazil and the other to West Africa. Their purpose was to photograph an eclipse of the sun. In these two expeditions were some of the ablest scientists of the day, including Sir Arthur Eddington. What was the occasion of this unwonted excitement among scientists?

In the year 1915 strange tidings had come out of Berlin. A German scientist, who had already established a notable reputation, announced new and revolutionary theories of astronomy and physics. It was a startling onslaught on accepted ideas.

He declared that Newton's law of gravitation was defective and that in certain particulars the axioms of Euclid's geometry were false. Then, most daring of all, he affirmed that the light from distant stars is bent when it passes through the gravitational field of the sun. Here was scientific heresy of the rankest sort—challenging, provocative. Three years of bitter warfare had to pass before these theories could be tested. The opportunity came in 1919. On May 29 of that year the scientists set up their instruments and cameras. The morning was dull and cloudy. As the hour of the eclipse drew nigh there was suddenly a rift in the

34

clouds and observations were made with the instruments and photographs were taken.

Anxiously the scientists awaited the development of the pictures. When at last they were ready and they gathered around to study them, there, surely enough, was plain, indisputable evidence of the displacement of star images caused by the bending of the light rays as they passed through the gravitational field of the sun. The news, within hours, was telegraphed all around the earth, and Albert Einstein, who made the venturesome prediction, was acclaimed the greatest mind that the world has known since the days of Sir Isaac Newton.

Little wonder that people are amazed by the spectacular advances of modern science. One can understand, too, how Thomas Huxley in the period of cocksureness that characterized nineteenth-century science should have been led to write: "Religion says that the just shall live by faith. Science says that the just shall live by verification." The great biologist overlooked the fact that religion, as well as science, has its postulates and its own methods of verification.

Had Huxley lived in our day, he would have heard some of the leaders of science declaring not only that religion shall live by verification, but that science shall walk by faith.

For instance, Dr. Max Planck, friend and collaborator with Einstein, wrote: "Science demands also the believing spirit. Anybody who has been seriously engaged in scientific work of any kind realizes that over the entrance to the gates of the Temple of Science are written these words: 'Ye must have faith.' It is a quality which the scientists cannot dispense with."

In support of Dr. Planck's contention, Einstein came forward to say that all physical science is based on a vast assumption: that the external world with which the scientist deals is real. "That assumption," Einstein affirms, "is not

gained by any form of reasoning, but by direct perception
—by a metaphysical belief, akin to faith."

Some people hold that the only kind of certainty a man
can know is that which results from the methods of exact
science. Science has limited itself to things that are subject
to analysis. It employs the telescope, the microscope, the
test tube, and other scientific paraphernalia. Let it be remembered, however, that scientific analysis is not the only
road to certainty. In the realm of values, there is trustworthy
knowledge to be gained. In fact, the total picture of man and
the universe is most comprehensive and accurate according
to the analysis of values.

In the year 1926 a chemist decided that he would analyze
the human body and establish its commercial value. In pic-
turesque language he gives us these facts: Take an average
man five feet ten inches tall, weighing 150 to 160 pounds,
and analyze him chemically. He will contain "enough fat
to make seven bars of soap; enough iron to make a nail of
medium size; enough sugar to fill a shaker; enough lime to
whitewash a chicken coop; enough phosphorus to make
2,200 match tips; enough magnesium for a dose of magnesia;
enough potassium to explode a toy cannon, together with
a little sulphur," and you have a man!

The sales value of these chemicals in 1926 was ninety-
eight cents, according to this scientist. I am sure that in
this day of inflationary prices it would be at least five dollars! This is an illustration of what might be called a quantitative analysis of man. He is a composite of iron, fat, sugar,
lime, phosphorus, magnesia, potassium, and sulphur, worth
five dollars. But have you accounted for man in this analysis?
Have you explained that strange creature who takes his
stand on this round ball of earth, speeding through the sky
at a velocity of a thousand miles a minute, and reaches out
to the uttermost parts of the universe laying hold of far-
distant stars, analyzing the elements of which they are composed, appraising them, weighing them, measuring them,

and asking himself: "How am I related to this vast universe? What is the origin of these amazing faculties that enable me to understand its laws, to harness its stupendous forces, and to have dominion over all the Creator's works? Is my mind not a small model of the infinite intelligence that brought all this into being?" Here is a mystery to which science possesses no key.

Plato, Augustine, Dante, Milton, Newton, Michelangelo, Raphael, Washington, David Livingstone—each of them five dollars' worth of chemicals! Now have you explained them?

Turning from the scientific analysis of man we invite the poet and dramatist to speak. He says: "What a piece of work is a man! how noble in reason! how infinite in faculty! in form and moving how express and admirable! in action how like an angel! in apprehension how like a god!" I affirm that Shakespeare has given us a far more adequate and comprehensive description of man than the scientist with his quantitative analysis.

In our time a note of humility has been sounded. J. Arthur Thomson, a leader of scientific thought in this century, wrote: "Every additional discovery we make reveals to us the widening circles of our own ignorance," and Dr. Robert A. Millikan adds: "Modern science of the real sort is slowly learning to walk humbly with its God." It is true that "The just shall live by faith." It is also true that this faith will issue in verification. Faith is a venture but it is a venture which in the here and now will result in triumphant vindication. It begins as an experiment; it ends as an experience.

Let me give you my favorite definition of faith: "It is a faculty by which we take a thing on trust in order to prove that it is true." Now just so long as faith remains in the arena of intellectual debate, it will always be possible to find counter-arguments. When, however, we turn from the arena of an academic discussion of faith to a present-day actual experience of the power of God in human lives, we pass from faith's venture to faith's verification.

One day in the long ago, as Jesus was walking in the Temple area in Jerusalem, he came face to face with a man who was blind from birth. The Master's heart was moved with compassion and he said to him: "Go and wash in the pool of Siloam and your sight will be restored." He challenged the blind man's faith; he called upon him to make a great venture. The man might have reasoned: "Why go to the pool of Siloam? How do I know that I am not setting forth on a fool's errand? Why should I make myself the laughingstock of all my friends?" Yet there was a strange accent of authority and power in the words of the Man who addressed him, so he went and washed in the pool of Siloam and returned seeing. The venture of faith resulted in verification.

It was then that the scribes and Pharisees saw the man and in their hostility to Jesus, they said to him: "Don't you see that this man has desecrated the Sabbath day in healing you? He is not a good man; he is a sinner. Put no trust in him."

Now, if the healed man had been content to let the discussion remain in the arena of intellectual debate, he could not have held his own with the learned doctors of the law. Instead, he turned from academic discussion to the appeal to experience, and said: "Whether he is a sinner or not, I know not, but one thing I know, whereas I was blind, now I see." There wasn't a man among them who could say a word against his testimony. The result of the venture of faith is always creative and transforming; it brings its reward in proportion to the measure of our faith.

When Dr. Elwood Worcester was carrying on his remarkable ministry among individuals in Boston, oftentimes Harvard students came to consult him. One day he was in the Appleton Chapel and a youth wandered in. When Dr. Worcester asked him about his religious life, the boy replied bitterly: "I came to Harvard to get away from that nonsense." When he was asked if he ever prayed, he said: "No, prayer is the act of a fool or an imbecile who likes to talk with himself."

Dr. Worcester was too wise a counselor not to recognize that the bitterness and scorn in the youth revealed his inner unhappiness, so he manifested no impatience or annoyance whatsoever. Then Dr. Worcester added: "Young man, you pride yourself on being scientific. Very well, I propose to you an experiment. I challenge you to set aside five minutes of each day for three weeks when, with all the earnestness you can command, you will ask God to reveal himself to you in power." The youth accepted the challenge.

Several weeks later Dr. Worcester received a letter from him. For the first week or more his skepticism had been confirmed. There was no response to his prayers. "Then," he said, "came a day when, crushed with discouragement and depression, I began to toy with the idea of suicide. I went off to my room alone and flung myself on my knees and prayed 'O God, help me, help me now,' and then waited. There came an unforgettable moment when my whole mind was filled with light. In that Divine light and joy all the darkness and bitterness of my life was swept away."

Said Dr. Worcester: "The power of God revealed in that youth gave him a new life's purpose, and at great sacrifice this Harvard student consecrated himself to the service of Christ." Like the man in ancient Jerusalem he could say: "One thing I know, that whereas I was blind, now I see."

During the last twenty-five years I have had interviews with thousands of persons and have seen the power of God transforming seemingly hopeless situations, lifting men and women out of moral defeat into victory, out of darkness into light, out of conflict and tension into calm and inner peace.

It is these experiences, not of theoretical religion, but of the power of the living God at work in human lives, that give one a certainty that not all the hostility of earth or of hell can shake.

So faith begins in venture, but it ends in verification; it begins in experiment, but it is confirmed by results.

> Then through the mid complaint of my confession
> Then through the pang and passion of my prayer
> Leaps with a start the shock of his possession,
> Thrills me and touches, and the Lord is there.

> Whoso hath felt the spirit of the highest
> Cannot confound nor doubt him nor deny
> Yea, with one voice, O World, tho' thou deniest
> Stand thou on that side, for on this am I.[1]

[1] F. W. Myers, "St. Paul." Used by permission of the Macmillan Co., publishers.

The Foundation of Life

*I had fainted, unless I had believed to see the
goodness of the Lord in the land of the living.*
—Ps. 27:13

MARCUS AURELIUS, a Roman Emperor of the second century,
was one of the noblest pagans of history. At a time when
corruption and self-indulgence were universal, he was un-
affected, self-denying, and pure.

Nevertheless, he found himself repeatedly crushed by
the burdens of state. Through all his writings there is a
melancholy strain suggesting the futility of life.

T. R. Glover, of Cambridge, estimating his character,
says: "He does not believe enough to be great."

Truly, our capacity to believe will determine very largely the effectiveness of our lives.

Dr. E. Griffith Jones put it like this: "All of us in the end
tend to become what we are in virtue of the operative beliefs of our life."

This is always a viewpoint of the Bible. The Psalmist
says: "I had fainted, unless I had believed to see the goodness
of the Lord in the land of the living."

The man who penned these words lived in a stormy
time. He found himself hedged about with adversities. He
had met crushing sorrows and disappointments. Life had
almost overwhelmed him. Looking back over the experiences
through which he had passed, he says: "I had fainted, unless
I had believed." The operative beliefs of his life saved him
from despair. Despite the contradictory evidence visible all

41

around him, he still believed in the Divine government of the world, and this faith garrisoned his heart with courage.

In the verse immediately following the words I have quoted, the psalmist reveals the manner in which his faith was kept alive and constantly nourished. "Wait on the Lord," he writes, "be of good courage, and he shall strengthen thine heart: wait, I say, on the Lord."

His secret was prayer. Through troublous days he never ceased to keep open the lines of communication with God. The limitless resources of the Eternal flowed through his heart, giving him the courage with which to face life.

We, too, are living in stressful and bewildering days. The nations of the world are faced with problems that baffle the best minds of our time. So far no principle of unity has been found. The great powers stand eying one another suspiciously, each with a hand resting on his sword. The East and the West are separated by ideological chasms so vast that some people have lost hope, saying: "They can never be bridged."

One has only to listen to discussions of the present world situation and of the prospects for the human race to know whether or not one is listening to people who possess faith.

A little time ago I talked with a man who is a trustee of one of the greatest universities in this nation. He has been intimately associated with the development of atomic energy. After discoursing for a little while on the destructive energies now put into the hands of man, he said: "As I review the history of the human race for the past six thousand years, I can see no hope that man will deal any more wisely with this problem than he has with those that have arisen in the past. I can't see even a gleam of light on the horizon so far as the survival of the human race is concerned." This brilliant man fairly dripped with pessimism. He was thoroughly depressed. I knew why his morale was so low, why he was so hopeless, why his heart failed him for fear.

I said to him: "In your review of the possibilities of the future you have left out the most important factor of all."

"What is that?" he asked.

I replied: "It is God. I cannot believe that the God who created man in his own image and likeness, endowing him with power, not only to unlock the secrets of the universe but also to hold fellowship with his creator, will now abandon man to self-destruction."

My friend shook his head sadly, and said: "I wish I had that much faith."

We have not by any means finished with our discussion, and, by the grace of God, some day he may have faith.

If there ever was a time in human history when faith was at a premium, it is now. Unbelief saps the courage of man, and cuts the nerve of every effort for human betterment.

The utter aimlessness to which the universe is reduced by pessimistic thinkers is revealed in the words of one of the skeptical writers of our time. He says: "Life has become in that total perspective which is philosophy a fitful breeding of human insects on earth, a planetary eczema which may soon be cured; nothing is certain except defeat and death."

No youth ever rose from reading sentiments like these with a passionate desire in his heart to build a world that will be a fit habitation for God's children. Truly, "I had fainted unless I had believed."

One evening last summer I was reading a book on the philosophy of humanism by an American author, when I came upon this conclusion: "We are alone in a terrifying and uncaring universe." Having read these words, I walked out into the night and looked up at the stars.

Not the least of the benefits of country life in the summertime is that we can see the stars again when we get away from the man-made lights of the city. There is something in the very atmosphere of the country that helps to restore one's balance and perspective.

Gazing up at thousands of shining points of light in the

dome of heaven, I found myself asking: "Do these stars look down from their cold, serene, passionless height utterly indifferent to the joys and sorrows of human existence? Is this universe in which man makes his home utterly uncaring for the human creature it has brought into existence, and has it no prospect for him but ultimate destruction; or can we believe that behind these 'swinging lanterns of eternity' is a purpose and a love that embraces all things?"

If the human race ever came to the point of believing that we are "alone in a terrifying and uncaring universe," then death would become the normal pursuit of man, for it would mean that all the labor and sacrifice that has been expended on behalf of others, all the onward progress of the race, all the tears that have been shed, all the sufferings that have been endured and the lives that have been laid down in the hope of bringing in a better day, will go for nothing, doomed to perish before "the trampling march of unconscious power."

From this bleak prospect we turn to where "the soul of the universe looks out through the eyes of Jesus Christ." In his life and teaching, in his faith and philosophy, we have the only satisfying answer to man's endless quest for truth. His revelation of the unseen God is summed up in the sublime words of the prayer he taught his disciples: "Our Father which art in heaven."

This faith preserves us from discouragement and despair, for it holds the promise of "the victory that overcometh the world."

A few years ago, in Town Hall, New York, Kirtley Mather, of Harvard University, with two other speakers, addressed a large audience of students and young people. He spoke rather hopefully about the future of mankind.

When the question period came, one of the students asked Professor Mather how he related his optimistic outlook on the future to the question of faith in God; did he believe in God? Professor Mather gave this reply: "I welcome the opportunity . . . to talk about God. As a man of science, as a geologist, I know quite definitely that there is an administration of the universe. Our world is not a world of chance and accident; it is an ordered world. . . . But that is not enough. Human nature yearns for a God of love. . . . Therefore, I, too, would couple the brotherhood of man with the fatherhood of God."

Here is a spiritual philosophy that the United Nations Organization desperately needs to give it unity of purpose and to undergird all its deliberations.

Christianity's only rival on a world scale today is the philosophy of Marxism. By its very nature its appeal is restricted. It is sectional, divisive, and has no place for God. By its very nature, it promotes discord rather than unity. It singles out one class, the proletariat, and would make it supreme.

The Christian philosophy, on the other hand, is inclusive. It emphasizes the brotherhood of man, but points out that human brotherhood possesses no significance whatsoever apart from the divine fatherhood. All movements, whatever their origin, that talk about the brotherhood of man while ignoring the fatherhood of God, are promoting an irrational creed.

If what the pessimists say were really true, and man is nothing more than "a beast that nourishes a blind life within the brain," if he is merely "a cosmic accident, a disease on the planet that will soon be cured," what basis is there for believing in human brotherhood? Life becomes a struggle for existence around a jungle waterhole. If man be no more than an animal, why should he not exploit, trample upon, victimize his fellow creature? May he not, in acting in this fashion, be fulfilling the inner law of his being?

Unalterably opposed to such a conception of life and man stands the teaching of Jesus. It must never be forgotten, however, that human brotherhood becomes an actuality only when we accept the reality of God's fatherhood.

The one who believes in God's government of the world and in a divine Purpose which runs like a golden thread through history, possesses a confidence that holds him steady in the face of discouraging reverses, for he knows that God is ultimately undefeatable in his purpose for his children. He does not faint because he believes.

What is true on a world scale is also true of the individual. Belief in God and an experiential knowledge of his divine power makes a man invincible in the face of adversity.

As William James phrases it: "Every sort of energy and endurance, of courage and capacity for handling life's evils is set free in those who have religious faith."

On one occasion a minister friend of mine was looking over some books in my library. He came upon a rationalist publication printed in London. He said: "Don't tell me that you subscribe to this magazine! It reeks with atheism."

I replied: "That is quite true. Nevertheless, I enjoy reading it. It is always helpful to read articles that set forth clearly, honestly, and frankly what is involved in the denial of God. I know no better argument for the necessity of faith."

I believe that one of the most effective illustrations I have used in an Easter sermon was drawn from the pages of this publication. It was a poem on the subject of death. The writer, an avowed atheist, pictured life as a blind process in an indifferent and purposeless universe. Death is "a sheer precipice behind which life drops into nothingness."

In the poem he begins to speak in words of tenderness of one whom death had taken but a few weeks before. In graphic and beautiful phrases he expresses loneliness, futility, and his despair in the loss of his wife whom he loved dearly.

I read that poem to a great congregation on Easter Sunday morning, and then turned from its bleak and desolate phrases to the blazing assurance of the Easter faith that this corruptible must put on incorruption, and this mortality

must put on immortality: "Then shall be brought to pass
the saying that is written, Death is swallowed up in victory.
O death, where is thy sting? O grave, where is thy victory? . . . Thanks be to God, which giveth us the victory
through our Lord, Jesus Christ."

Here are the alternatives, and we must choose for ourselves: It is either God or no God. Either there is a Helper
and a Friend beside us on life's pilgrimage, or else we are
alone in a friendless and uncaring universe. Either death is
the opening of a door to our Father's house on high, where
the unfulfilled purposes and half-realized ideals of life advance to full fruition in that life of heavenly service, or
else death is a blind alley, inexorably ending all the highest
hopes of man, burying them amidst the ashes of a dying
universe.

The loftiness or the pettiness of your life on earth will
be determined by the choice you make of these alternatives.
The results of your decision will extend beyond time into
eternity.

The venture of faith demanded by a positive decision will
eventually bring its own verification. This was the experience
of the psalmist. He had believed to see the goodness of the
Lord in the land of the living, and his faith was not disappointed. He waited on God and drew from the divine resources the courage and strength with which to face life
without fear.

We all need a reference beyond the stresses and strains
of this mortal life, that we may draw upon the quietness
and strength of eternity.

In the Greenwich Observatory, where the world's time
is kept, the clocks are mounted on concrete piers which are
sunk deep into the earth to avoid vibration. They are housed
in a room kept at a constant temperature. Every twenty-
eight seconds they are wound automatically, but despite all
these precautions, they do not keep perfect time. Each night
they are corrected by checking the movement of the earth

on its axis in relation to fixed stars millions of light years away. Man gets his true time only from the sky.

This is a parable of our spiritual life. God has planted eternity and immortality within every human breast, and man's fullest life is achieved only in fellowship with him.

"Thou hast made us to incline to Thee," said Augustine, "and our hearts are restless and tormented until in Thee they find their peace."

Then "Wait on the Lord: be of good courage, and he shall strengthen thine heart: wait, I say, on the Lord."

Allegiance to a Dream

And when he was come near, he beheld the city,
and wept over it, saying, If thou hadst known, even
thou, at least in this thy day, the things which be-
long unto thy peace! but now they are hid from
thine eyes.   —LUKE 19:41-42

ON AN APRIL morning long, long ago in far-off Judea, a
little band of pilgrims were making their way toward the
crest of the Mount of Olives. They had left behind them
the friendly home of Bethany under its sheltering palms
and were journeying to Jerusalem. They were not alone for
the highways were crowded with pilgrims as the greatest
Feast-day of the year was drawing nigh and every patriotic
Jew wished to celebrate the Passover in the capital city of
the nation.

This year the interest of the pilgrims was at fever pitch.
The very air was electric with excitement. The whole land
was on tiptoe of expectancy, for the news had gone abroad
that the Prophet of Nazareth would appear in Jerusalem in
the midst of the Feast; that he would proclaim himself
Messiah, overthrowing the power of Rome and casting out
the worldly-minded priests who had usurped the functions
of religion.

Even the disciples came under the spell, and they eagerly
watched the Master's face as they set out on the highway.

Early that morning two of their number had mysteriously
disappeared. When they returned leading a young colt,
the enthusiasm of the disciples knew no bounds.

49

Even Jesus seemed to have been caught in the upsurge
of triumphant joy, for he permitted them to put their garments on the back of the colt and set him thereon. And now
as they moved forward in triumphal procession, more and
more pilgrims were attracted to the scene until Jesus was
in the center of a vast multitude of rejoicing Galileans.
Instantly they recognized the symbolic significance of
his act. They were all familiar with the prophecy of
Zechariah: "Rejoice greatly, O daughter of Zion; shout, O
daughter of Jerusalem; behold, thy King cometh unto thee:
he is just, and having salvation; lowly, and riding upon
an ass, and upon a colt the foal of an ass. . . . And he shall
speak peace unto the heathen: and his dominion shall be
from sea even to sea, and from the river even unto the ends
of the earth."

The multitude preceding him down the mountainside
broke into songs of rejoicing: "Hosanna; Blessed is he that
cometh in the name of the Lord: Blessed be the kingdom of
our father David, that cometh in the name of the Lord:
Hosanna in the highest." Breaking off branches of the palm
trees they waved them in unison, keeping time to the music
of their song.

Here is revealed a dramatic about-face on the part of
Jesus! For months in the course of his ministry, he had
shunned publicity. Whenever he performed his miracles of
healing, invariably he demanded that the matter be kept
secret. When Peter declared that he was the Messiah, the
Son of the living God, Jesus said: "See that thou tell no man
this." After the feeding of the five thousand, when they
sought to take him by force and make him king, he slipped
away quietly into the solitude of the mountains and escaped
them.

But now apparently he is courting publicity. He arranged
to have the ass's colt on which he rode to Jerusalem. He
does not restrain the enthusiasm of his disciples. He has
become the center of a tremendous popular demonstration.

The Pharisees, sensing this change, go to Jesus and say: "Master, rebuke thy disciples. Tell them to be silent." Jesus answered: "I tell you that, if these should hold their peace, the stones would immediately cry out."

What is the explanation of this strange change of attitude? There can be but one valid interpretation—he is about to offer himself to the whole nation. If he is rejected, scorned, and crucified, it will not be a thing done in a corner. The whole nation, and eventually the whole world, will know about it. So he comes to the capital at the time of the greatest Feast—not secretly, not furtively—but openly in broad daylight, in triumphal procession, acclaimed as the Messiah.

The city of Jerusalem is situated on a rocky plateau 2,500 feet above the level of the sea. The eastern side descends swiftly to the Valley of Kidron. Opposite the city is the Mount of Olives, the crest of which is 200 feet higher than the capital. There is one point in the downward descent toward Jerusalem at which the whole city bursts suddenly into view. Many a traveler has reined in his horse at this memorable spot and looked upon the scene with feelings too deep for words.

H. V. Morton, author of *In the Footsteps of the Master*, says that he stood at this unforgettable place where Jesus had halted and saw the city before his eyes. It seemed to him "like a lion couched in the sun, watchful, vindictive, ready to kill."

Here the procession came to a standstill, and Jesus stood, and looked out over the city that he loved, the city of which he had said: "O Jerusalem, Jerusalem, thou that killest the prophets, and stonest them which are sent unto thee, how often would I have gathered thy children together, even as a hen gathereth her chickens under her wings, and ye would not!"

He sees the massive ramparts, the proud towers, the lordly palaces rising terrace upon terrace to the magnificent home of Herod the Great. Suddenly the shouting ceased, the palms were lowered, a hush of wondering silence fell upon the multitudes as their eyes were fastened upon the face of Jesus. He broke into loud lamentations: "If thou hadst known, even thou, at least in this thy day, the things which belong unto thy peace! but now they are hid from thine eyes."

The multitude saw only the glittering City of Herod and Tiberius, but Jesus saw down the vista of half a century the beloved City degraded from her lofty heights—her proud towers shattered, her battlements overthrown, her golden sanctuary polluted, and the hillsides covered with a forest of crosses, with their writhing victims, and on the crest of the city, the banner of the Roman Conqueror Titus flying triumphantly.

Yes, and he saw more than this. He saw the tragedy that would precede the destruction of that great City. He saw his own rejection and crucifixion. Far below in the valley the olive trees were flinging broad shadows over green Gethsemane, in whose somber depths he was to spend an hour of agony and bloody sweat and tears. He saw, too, the roof of Pilate's judgment hall where he would stand alone —mocked, jeered at and spat upon, not one voice lifted up in his defense, not one friend beside him, arraigned in the purple robe and the crown of thorns. And beyond the city he saw rising a hilltop—menacing and ugly, in the form of a skull—and in troubled imagination he saw three crosses rising on Golgotha!

And yet he would not turn back. It was for this that he steadfastly set his face to go to Jerusalem, because he believed it to be his Father's will.

It seemed so long, long ago when as a lad he often wandered to the rim of the hills amid which Nazareth lay and climbing to their summit looked down into the valleys, bloodstained by many an ancient battle, and far below on the highways he watched the caravans with their merchandise and slaves—men and women bought and sold like sheep. Oftentimes he watched the sunlight flashing back from Roman shields and spears as the soldiers returned from some mission of plunder.

And always he dreamed a wonderful dream of taking this world with its sorrow, its exploitation of man by man, and its sins, and lifting it up to the very throne of the heavenly Father. He dreamed that one day this world would become God's world. But as he went forth on his ministry, little by little he learned the bitter truth that men would not accept God's rule—that even as they had stoned and killed so many of God's messengers, so too they would kill him. As the writer to the Hebrews says: "Though he were a Son, yet learned he obedience by the things which he suffered."

For the truth broke in upon him that somehow his death would make men see the horror of sin and the wonder of God's redeeming love, until one day caught up by the glory of this vision, he cried aloud: "And I, if I be lifted up from the earth, will draw all men unto me."

And at another time: "No man taketh my life from me, but I lay it down of myself."

Strange how that Man on the cross has never ceased to grip the minds and hearts of men. I was in Russia in the days when it was the prime object of the government to blot out every vestige of religion in the land. The famous St. Isaac's Cathedral had been turned into an anti-religious museum. I walked along with a crowd of peasants and workers there, and listened to the atheistic lecturer talking to them. He pointed to some pictures of the heavens and said that this scientific evidence disproved the existence of God. Then he led us to a coffin in which was a half-decayed body and said that this body disproved faith in immortality. Finally, he showed us a huge picture of Jesus. In the foreground was a platoon of soldiers shooting down workers, while in the background Jesus stood with his hands lifted up in benediction upon this tragic spectacle. The lecturer said:

"Jesus was one of them—one of the capitalists. He was an exploiter, too. You must learn to hate him."

Then we left the Anti-Religious Museum and went down the street a few steps to the Hermitage—the greatest art gallery in all Russia. Again I followed the workers and the peasants. They walked through the gallery looking with uncomprehending eyes on the great works of art before them. Suddenly the crowd came face to face with a huge painting of Jesus on the cross. Every man of them stopped dead still in the presence of that painting. The lecturer was not with them now. They were without a leader. I watched their faces. One could almost read their thoughts.

"If the Man on the cross was an exploiter, why did the authorities kill him? He doesn't look like a cruel man. There is something very kindly in his face and his hands are calloused with toil like ours. Why, of course, he was a carpenter! And if he was an exploiter and an enemy of the people, what gain did he have to show at the end? He had nothing save these poor garments he is dressed in. And there is something very Godlike in his face as he forgives those who are crucifying him."

I saw a look of comprehension come into the face of the foremost workman as he reached up his hand and laid hold of his tattered cap and pulled it off, twisting it in his hands, and watching the face of the Man on the cross. In a moment every head was bared. And I seemed to hear a voice that said: "And I, if I be lifted up from the earth, will draw all men unto me."

Once again we are back in Pilate's Judgment Hall. The soldiers are there, and the mob, and the priests and the lone Prisoner standing in kingly solitude, with seas of hate surging around him—the one calm, majestic personality in all that fevered scene. He is wearing the purple robe and the crown of thorns as Pilate enters. Pointing at the Man of Nazareth, he says: "Ecce homo!" "Behold the man."

"That 'Ecce Homo' of Pontius Pilate has drawn the eyes

of all generations to that marred visage and lo! as we look, the shame is all gone. It is lifted from Him and it has fallen on Pilate, the soldiers, the priests and the mob. His outflashing glory has burned away every speck of disgrace and tipped that crown of thorns with a hundred points of flaming brightness."

And ever and always before my eyes I see a huge towering cross with great arms stretched out to the east and the west, to the rising and the setting sun and on that cross my God still hangs in his work of redemption: "Is it nothing to you, all ye that pass by? behold, and see if there be any sorrow like unto my sorrow!"

Will you not give him your allegiance and your love? He is challenging us to fulfill his dream and make this world God's world, God's Kingdom of justice, and freedom and peace. The spirit of his Cross is the hope of the world.

> In the cross of Christ I glory,
>   Towering o'er the wrecks of time;
> All the light of sacred story
>   Gathers round its head sublime.

FROM DOUBT INTO FAITH

Science--and Religious Faith

> *If ye continue in my word, then are ye my disciples indeed; and ye shall know the truth, and the truth shall make you free.*   —John 8:31-32

ONE OF THE regrettable episodes of history for the past four hundred years has been the so-called conflict between science and religion. It is all the more to be deplored because it was entirely unnecessary.

An able investigator in this field, Andrew D. White, who for twenty years was the president of Cornell University, devoted a quarter of a century's study to this subject. He has summarized his findings in these words: "There never has been a conflict between science and religion; there has been a conflict between science and dogmatic theology."

Let us examine these words "religion" and "theology" to understand their significance. Religion has been defined as "the possession or practice of religious beliefs." Theology is "the formulation of religious knowledge and belief—the intellectual presentation of the subject matter of religion." Now, religion precedes theology. There could be no theology without religion, just as there could be no science of botany unless there were plants.

The conflict, therefore, never has been between the rank and file of Christian believers and science, but between theological leaders and the scientists. In earlier years, the warfare was one-sided, since all the power and authority was in the hands of churchmen. As the centuries passed, science

59

began striking back with increasing effectiveness and the conflict became intensified and ever more bitter.

The function of science and theology had never been clearly defined. They operate in separate and distinct areas, with some common territory in which they overlap, but this fact was not known until after there had been nearly four centuries of struggle and opposition.

The conflict opened in the year 1543, when Copernicus published his great work setting forth the heliocentric theory of the universe: that the sun is the center of our solar system and that our earth and the other planets revolve around it. At a later date Galileo demonstrated the rotation of the earth on its axis.

Looking back over the centuries, it seems very strange to us that theologians should have become excited and angry at these scientific revelations, because they gave to man a vaster and nobler concept of God. No longer would they have to think of him in limited ways. As a satirist put it, "God does not have to say to the sun every morning 'Get up and do it again.'"

Unfortunately, however, the theologians of the seventeenth century were obsessed with a vast misconception, an error that has persisted down to our own time. They believed that the Bible has the dual function of teaching spiritual truth and recording definitive scientific facts. At this point most of the conflicts and antagonisms began.

The Sacred Congregation at Rome met with Pope Pius the Fifth in 1616, to consider the proposition that "the sun is the center around which the earth revolves." They declared that this proposition "is absurd; it is false in theology, and heretical, because absolutely contrary to Holy Scripture." Yet in every parochial school in the world today this doctrine is being taught.

John Calvin joined the fray by denouncing the teaching of Galileo, that the earth revolves on its axis. He thought he had demolished the scientists when he quoted the first verse of the ninety-third psalm: "The world also is established that it cannot be moved."

Even the devout and saintly Isaac Newton, one of the most godly and reverent of men, did not escape the theological onslaught. They said "He has dethroned Providence —substituting gravity for God." But today religious people of every nation are proud to honor the memory of Isaac Newton.

One of the deplorable results of the theologian's efforts to make the Bible a textbook of science is that in the ensuing melee the deep, abiding, spiritual truths of the Scriptures were trampled upon. Some people in the seventeenth century were so affrighted lest the revelations of science would destroy their faith, that they could not be persuaded to look at the heavens through a telescope. Their counterpart is seen in the modern-day Christians who greatly fear that the giant 200-inch-lens telescope which will soon be in operation may reveal astronomical secrets that will militate against religious faith.

I stood one night on the summit of Mt. Wilson, California, and looked through the most powerful telescope in the world. It was turned upon the constellation of Orion, which can be seen any winter night in the Southern sky. The telescope was directed at the star known as Betelgeuse. I was looking at that marvelous flaming body in the heavens, when the astronomer standing beside me said: "We measured Betelgeuse quite accurately in 1920 with the interfermometer, and we found that it is 260,000,000 miles in diameter." He continued: "Compare that with our earth, with its 8,000 miles in diameter, and it will give you an idea of its immensity." Then, pausing a moment, he said: "It is 32,500 times bigger than our world," and when I gasped with amazement, the astronomer added: "You see, science is compelling us to think great thoughts of God."

Now, it is not the business of science to teach religious truths, just as it is not the function of the Bible to teach science. Nevertheless, science by its revelation of the immensities of space and all pervading orderliness and harmony of the universe is teaching us larger conceptions of the Creator and his activities.

Jesus said: "Ye shall know the truth, and the truth shall make you free."

The greatest liberating force in the world is truth—the truth about the universe and the truth about God. Both science and religion have the same goal of truth which they approach from different pathways, and anyone who follows the path of truth, whether it be in scientific investigation or in religious pursuits, will find God at his journey's end.

It is hard for people to realize that there is no such object, entity or concrete reality as science. Science is simply a well-tested method of compilation, verification, and observation. It is the collection of data, the verifying of it, and the comparison of similar results gathered where conditions are the same.

One thing a true scientist will never do: distort a fact to fit it into theory. They build their theories out of the facts as they observe them. The method of scientists is empirical, that is, it is by observation and experimentation, but there are many facets of reality that cannot be known by the method of science. J. Arthur Thomson acknowledges this. He says: "Science fishes in the sea of reality with a special kind of net—scientific methods—but there may be much in the unfathomed sea which the meshes of the scientific net cannot catch."

Take a scientist to the seaside and say to him: "What do you see?" Looking at the water he replies: "Basically, I observe hydrogen and oxygen in combination—eleven plus per cent hydrogen by weight and oxygen eighty-eight plus per cent by weight. Our chemical description of it is H_2O."

Then you take a poet to the ocean side, Lord Byron for instance. You ask: "What do you see?" He answers:

> Dark-heaving, endless and sublime,
> The image of Eternity—the throne of the invisible.
> Thou goest forth dread, fathomless, alone.

Take a religious seer or prophet to view the ocean and ask him: "What thoughts come to you when you look out upon the deep?" He replies:

> They that go down to the sea in ships and do business in
>   great waters,
> These see the works of the Lord and his wonders in the deep.

Now the poetic and religious approach is just as valid as the scientific and just as revealing of reality.

The scientific method of experiment and analysis is good in many fields, but has its shortcomings. Keats rebelled at the manner in which it robbed him of the rainbow's glory. It cannot be applied universally. Take, for instance, the business of romantic love. I shouldn't advise young people to employ the method of experimentation, observation, and analysis in this field. Used exclusively it will result in failure. A young student visited regularly the girl of his choice, and she welcomed his attentions until she discovered that he was so scientifically minded that as he whispered his endearments in her ear he kept his finger on her pulse to test her reactions. That is the scientific method, and it leaves much to be desired.

Sometimes poets become indignant at the method of analysis carried to extremes. Wordsworth writes:

> A fingering slave,
> One that would peep and botanize
> Upon his mother's grave.

The endless dissecting techniques of science against which the poets rebel would analyze a mother's face until its lines of loving solicitude are reduced to a matter of bones and muscles, sweat glands and nerve ends, overlaid by a covering of epidermis. Truly, there are more facts in life than are embraced in many a scientist's philosophy.

Fifty years ago the intellectuals were shouting for the release of science from the domination of religion. Today every thoughtful person is becoming frightened at the revelations of science.

One of the best-known scientists of our time, Julian Huxley, has described the situation: "Humanity is rather like an irresponsible and mischievous child who has been presented with a set of machine tools, a box of matches, and a supply of dynamite." The only trouble with this scientist's figure of speech is that it is not sufficiently descriptive.

The scientists themselves are deeply disturbed today. I spent several hours with one of the physicists closely associated with atomic research, and he is greatly concerned about recent developments. Every scientist knows that unless man develops moral and spiritual restraints, he will perish in the atomic fires that science has kindled. He must learn obedience to the laws of God and to the Divine will, for only then can he live at peace with his fellows. Each of us has a part to play and an influence to exert to this end.

"If ye continue in my word," said Christ, "then are ye my disciples indeed, and ye shall know the truth, and the truth shall make you free."

Amid the bewilderment and confusion of our time the personality of Jesus towers in solitary majesty as the world's only hope, for he is "the way, the truth, and the life."

On the day when the British, Canadian, and American scientists cracked wide open the inexhaustible arsenal of solar energy, the scientists led us to the verge of a precipice into whose abyss we dare not look. Godless science and godless nations may lay waste the world, but a science that becomes the ally and the handmaiden of religion, and that lays its trophies at the feet of Jesus Christ may well become the harbinger of a new and better day for all mankind.

The Origin of the Universe

*In the beginning God created the heaven and
the earth.* —GEN. 1:1

THE GREATEST disservice rendered to the Christian faith in
the last four centuries has been done, not by the enemies,
but by the friends, of our religion. A false conception of
the Bible has alienated tens of thousands of intellectually
honest young men and women, and driven them reluctantly
into skeptical attitudes and ideas.

The doctrine that the Bible is a textbook of science has
done incalculable harm and has caused immense confusion
in the minds of multitudes. It has enabled skeptics, such as
Robert Ingersoll, to hold the Bible and Christianity up to
contempt and derision since it was not difficult for him and
for others to prove that this contention is not true. But
who reads Ingersoll today? He is hopelessly out of date, and
he is out of date because we have laid hold upon sounder and
truer conceptions of the Bible. When that happened, his
argument collapsed of its own weight.

It is dangerous and reckless for any responsible Christian
leader to say: "If science should prove this doctrine true,
the Bible is false." Yet that statement has been made again
and again in the last four hundred years. Not only the
Church of Rome, but some of the Reformers, also, said that
if the earth moves in an orbit around the sun, the Bible is
untrue; if the earth spins on its axis, the Bible is untrust-
worthy; if there is a mysterious force in the universe known

65

as gravity which holds the planets in their orbits, then God has been dethroned.

Copernicus and Galileo proved the first two propositions which are accepted universally today. The third has also been received and taught throughout the whole civilized world.

When religious leaders resort to sweeping and irresponsible statements, they discredit the faith which they seek to defend.

The pioneers of scientific research, such as Copernicus, Galileo, Newton, and others, were all men of profound religious faith and blameless life; yet, they were bitterly persecuted.

Even after the death of Copernicus, his relatives didn't dare inscribe his achievements on his tombstone, lest his grave be desecrated. On it was carved a simple prayer which reflected the Christian humility of the great scientist: "I ask not the grace accorded to Paul, nor that given to Peter; give me only the favor which Thou didst show to the thief on the cross."

All such slogans as "We must choose geology or Genesis"; "We must choose science or religion" are mischievous and harmful, for they present a false antithesis. It is "geology *and* Genesis"; it is "science *and* God."

Kepler uttered a profound truth when he said to his friends that night after night as he looked through his telescope and read the secrets of the heavens: "I think God's thoughts after him." Yet misguided men and women claim that we must go to the Bible for a knowledge of science. They have sought to wrest from its chapters a truer knowledge of the method and manner of creation than science offers us.

Now, the absurd lengths to which some theologians have gone is revealed in the writings of Dr. John Lightfoot, Chancellor of Cambridge University. He lived in the seventeenth century. The venerable doctor declared that, after a profound study of the sacred scriptures, he established the following facts: "Heaven and earth, centre and circumference, were created all together in the same instant and clouds full of water;" and that "this work took place and man was created by the Trinity on October 23, 4004 B.C. at nine o'clock in the morning." There were people in his day ready to fight to the death anyone who challenged this fantastic assertion. Unfortunately for Dr. Lightfoot's theory, within a few years it was established that by the year 4004 B.C. there were ancient and highly developed civilizations flourishing in the land of Egypt and in Ur of the Chaldees, the home of Abraham.

One wonders why people who look to the Bible for science do not stop to ask themselves this question: "If the Bible, and especially the Book of Genesis, teaches science, what is the period of scientific knowledge with which it deals?" Is it the old Hebrew cosmograph? The Ptolemaic concept of the universe? The Copernican theory? The Newtonian concept or is it Einstein's relativity?

If the human race were dependent on the Bible for its scientific knowledge, then, for the greater part of history, it would either be an outmoded book or an inscrutable mystery according as it taught older or newer science. The strength and glory of the Bible lies in the fact that its function is not to impart scientific information, but to reveal God to man and to set forth a progressive spiritual revelation of the Divine Creator, culminating in the incarnation of Jesus Christ, his Son.

What basically are the affirmations of the Bible, and particularly of the Book of Genesis, respecting the universe?

The first is this: The world, with its harmony and orderliness and rationality and all the teeming life that crowds our planet, came into existence through the creative activity of Almighty God.

Secondly: The goal and crown of creation and of the divine activity is centered in man, made in the image of his

Maker, and gifted with the power of holding fellowship with his great Originator.

These affirmations have nothing to do with the manner, that is with the "*how*" of creation. Such is the prerogative of science. Religion answers the questions: *Whence? Whither? Why?* These are its field of inquiry. Into these issues of spiritual reality science has no vocation to inquire.

Nevertheless, scientists themselves tell us that by using the scientific method of observation and experimentation, they have arrived at the same place as the seers and prophets of the ages—the august presence of God. Many of these scientists are the leaders in their respective fields of research.

Sir Oliver Lodge, the eminent British physicist, writes: "Science does not deal with origins—not ultimate origins. It takes the universe as a going concern and tries to explore it."

Employing the scientific method what does he find?

"In the beginning—and certainly there was a beginning to the solar system and the world—there was the brooding of a divine Spirit, an infinite Mind at work, planning and executing."

One year before I came to the city of New York it was my very great privilege to welcome to my pulpit in Winnipeg one of the greatest present-day scientists. A congregation of twenty-five hundred heard his address, with amplifiers carrying his message to halls of the church. He was Robert A. Millikan, who had been awarded the Nobel prize for his tremendous achievement in isolating the electron. Dr. Millikan emphatically asserted that there is not a shred of evidence that science has ever undermined a basic religious truth, and that science and religion are sister forces working together for the advancement and the uplift of mankind. He has ever been the opponent of destructive skepticism.

"The atheist," says Dr. Millikan, "is irrational and unscientific, because he asserts that there is nothing behind or inherent in all the phenomena of nature except blind force . . .

denying as he does any purpose or trend in nature . . ." and any such denial, says Dr. Millikan, is a direct contradiction of the findings of modern science.

Now, I am not competent to evaluate the scientific methods by which men like Millikan and Sir Oliver Lodge and others reach these conclusions, but I am encouraged and strengthened in my own convictions to discover that they have arrived at the same point as I by an altogether different route.

What a magnificent panorama of creation is drawn for us in the Book of Genesis! It is sheer prose poetry, concluding time and again with the refrain "and God saw that it was good." The description of the universe is simple and primitive. If you wish to picture it symbolically, think of the old-fashioned butter dish that used to adorn our tables. The flat plate represents the earth, and over the flat earth was the dome of heaven, like the cover of the butter dish. On the underpart of the dome were set the stars and the moon and the sun, to give light on the earth. Under this vault stood man looking up at the solid firmament filled with lights like lamps suspended from the dome of a cathedral. There were three oceans, one that surrounded the flat earth, the other above the solid dome of the firmament, with openings through which rain fell upon the earth, and the third was underneath the earth. "And God said, let there be a firmament in the midst of the waters, and let it divide the waters from the waters. . . . And God made the firmament, and divided the waters which were under the firmament from the waters which were above the firmament; and it was so."

The inspired writer of the Book of Genesis, using the thought-forms and the language of his day, has taught the human race an imperishable spiritual truth, that God is behind all creation, "the brooding of a divine Spirit, an infinite Mind at work, planning and executing."

Remember that precious gifts are sometimes brought to

us in ancient wrappings. We may be devoutly thankful that religious revelation is not concerned with the changing postulates of science.

Just at the moment Einstein's conception of a limited universe and curved space holds the field, but he would be a bold man who would dare affirm that this conception will not be profoundly modified, and, perhaps, even completely rejected within the next fifty years.

Science changes from age to age but the Bible presents spiritual truths that belong to the ages and the eternities. They will never change for they are a revelation of the will and purpose of the living God. In this Book, above all things else, is enshrined the personality and the message of Jesus Christ, God's final revelation to man. Here is one of the imperishable spiritual truths that he uttered: "Thou shalt love the Lord thy God with all thy heart and with all thy soul and with all thy mind and with all thy strength; and thy neighbor as thyself."

Heaven and earth shall pass away, but these words shall not pass away and this law shall not be abrogated. When the memory of Ptolemy, Copernicus, Galileo, Kepler, Newton, Darwin, and Einstein will have faded from the minds of men, this spiritual law set forth by our Lord will shine forth with ever greater brilliance, as a beacon of truth, and as the goal and watchword of a united and peace-loving world. Whatever be the teaching of science as to the manner of creation in God's unfolding plan, remember always these majestic words from the opening chapter of the Bible: "In the beginning, God"—"the brooding of a Divine Spirit and infinite Mind at work, planning and executing"; at every stage of the process, God; in the end God, bringing the vast drama to one glorious and resplendent consummation.

> That God, which ever lives and loves,
> One God, one law, one element
> And one far-off divine event
> To which the whole creation moves.

The Origin of Man

*And the Lord God formed man of the dust of
the ground, and breathed into his nostrils the breath
of life; and man became a living soul.—*GEN. 2:7

THE ACCOUNT OF creation in Genesis is not chronological,
biological, or geological; in no sense of the word is it an
attempt to give a scientific description of creation. It is
a simple story, couched in the thought-forms of the people
of the day in which it was written.

When one teaches a child, one employs words that the
child understands. The story of creation in the book of
Genesis was written for the childhood of our race. Nevertheless, as we have it, it contains a profound spiritual
message, and with this we are dealing each week.

Whoever cannot believe that the record of the book of
Genesis is inspired unless it teaches scientific information,
has not learned the first principles of divine revelation.

How swiftly science changes its teachings from hypothesis
to hypothesis, from theory to theory! During the first decade
of this century, in all colleges and schools the theory of
gravitation was taught. We were all brought up on Newton's
falling apple. We believed that his theory was as firmly
grounded as truth itself. Then came Einstein. He said we
must profoundly modify our concept of gravitation. He
even dared to offer a new explanation of the falling apple.
"It fell," he said, "not because there was a mysterious force
pulling it downward, but because space is curved by the
presence of the great mass of the earth, and the apple took

71

the line of least resistance." If you throw a handful of marbles on the floor of a room, and you discover that they all run to the center, it might be that a mysterious force is attracting them. A more likely explanation, however, is that the floor is curved toward the center.

But Einstein goes beyond this. He startled the scientists by declaring that we are living in a finite universe. If a projectile were fired into space, with enough energy back of it to carry it on indefinitely, it would come right back to the place where it started.

Now the mathematicians are beginning to calculate the distance in light years around the majestic curve of the entire universe.

Sir Arthur Eddington says that light traveling at 186,000 miles per second will complete the circuit of the universe in one billion years. Then he adds: "If this is finitude, it is the kind of finitude which bludgeons the mind into stupefaction."

We had thought we were beginning to understand the universe, or that at least we saw a glimmer of light, with the steadying influence of Newton's law of gravitation, but now Einstein plunges us into bewilderment again.

You may recall that, on Newton's birthplace in England, is a tablet which bears two lines from Alexander Pope:

> Nature and nature's laws lay hid in night.
> God said, "Let Newton be," and all was light!

but J. C. Squire has added to that a satirical and humorous couplet:

> It did not last: the Devil howling "Ho!
> Let Einstein be," restored the *status quo*.

How true are the words of one of our ablest scientists, Dr. Whitney: "The best scientists have to recognize that they are just kindergarten fellows playing with mysteries; our ancestors were and our descendants will be."

We ought to be grateful that the Bible does not deal with the changing postulates of science, and that its message is not cast in the ever-altering scientific mold, but is based upon abiding spiritual truth.

When we turn to the book of Genesis and read its account of the creation of man, we are not surprised to find that it is altogether devoid of scientific teaching. It is a simple, primitive, poetic, and profoundly religious record of man's origin. "And the Lord God formed man of the dust of the ground, and breathed into his nostrils the breath of life; and man became a living soul." In other words, man is composed of dust and divinity. His body has come from the dust, and it will return to the dust again.

Scientists have demonstrated that all of the elements found in the body of man come from the dust of the ground that he tramples beneath his feet. The Genesis account pictures God molding the body of man very much as a potter molds a vessel—of clay and water. It is a primitive conception for the primitive people to whom it was first given, but that ancient story enshrines a dynamic truth— that man is divinity as well as dust; that God breathed into him his own spirit and made him in his own image. The divine Image is not to be found in the body of man, but in his mind and spirit.

Scientists have written a great deal in the past seventy-five years about the physical kinship of man with all the rest of creation. Even the book of Genesis confirms that man and the animals had the same origin, that they all spring from the dust, but the Bible doesn't stop there. It goes on to affirm the divine origin of man's spirit.

The anatomists, the biologists, the physiologists, the embriologists have each in turn produced evidence that testifies to man's kinship with the rest of creation. The last word has not yet been spoken on that subject.

One has only to study the distinct cleavage of thought among the scientists themselves to see how diverse are the conceptions they hold of man's origin. For instance, read the works of Darwin and then read the views of Henry Fairfield Osborn, the American scientist, and you will see how diametrically opposed they are in several important areas.

In the meanwhile, intelligent Christians will await the report of the scientists with equanimity, composure, and without a trace of fear. No true Christian is ever afraid of science. He will not fear what any branch of learning may reveal. If the time ever comes where science can produce evidence of the route of man's physical origin—evidence which can be conclusively and incontrovertibly proved, the intelligent Christian will accept the result without a tremor of anxiety, because religion is not concerned with that which is of the earth earthy, but with that which is "likest God within the soul." Whatever be the physical route by which man has arrived at his present stature, his responsibilities remain undiminished, his rights unimpaired, and his immortal hopes unclouded.

That man has been made in the image of God is abundantly proved by his remarkable mental and spiritual endowments. When anyone intelligently studies a painting such as, for instance, the *Sistine Madonna*, by Raphael, there is always a communion of mind of the beholder with that of the artist who painted the picture. Unless there is a kinship between them, it is a waste of time to try to find what the artist's message is.

Likewise, as man looks out upon creation, there is a communion between his mind and the mind of the Creator—a kinship and understanding. God's laws, God's work, the harmony and the rationality of the universe, bring to man a thrill of joy comparable to the divine rapture recorded in the Book of Genesis: "And God saw everything that he had made, and behold it was very good."

The British scientist, Sir James Jeans, is aware of this affinity, for he wrote: "The universe shows evidence of a designing or controlling power that has something in common with our own individual minds."

Has it ever occurred to you that the universe never would have been complete without man? If man had not emerged and looked out upon it, the universe would have remained blind to its own marvels and its own beauty. Man provides the eyes with which the universe beholds and enjoys itself. Until man came, there was no creature in all the created universe that enjoyed the wonder of it. The glory of the morning broke upon many a lovely valley, the dew sparkled like diamonds on the grass, the mountain peaks towered majestically, holding up to heaven their burden of untrampled snows, and prairie sunsets flamed in scarlet splendor across the Western skies, like the trailing garments of God, but no eye beheld it and no heart bowed in reverence. And God said in effect: "Let us make man in our own image, after our own likeness, with power to behold the universe and to see that it is good." So God created man in his own image, with the capacity of enjoying and appreciating beauty, and with a mind whose thoughts "wander through eternity."

Then came a night when a spiritually minded man looked up thoughtfully to the starry sky. Feelings of awe and reverence swept over him, and he said: "When I behold thy heavens—the works of thy fingers, and the moon and the stars which Thou has ordained, what is man that thou are mindful of him? Thou hast made him but a little lower than God." As the Creator beheld the awakening spirit of man the heart of God was glad.

Now we see man with ever-growing intelligence standing on this little ball of earth, looking out into the vast expanse of space, measuring the distant suns and planets with the interfermometer, weighing them by means of the laws of physics, analyzing their chemical composition with the spectroscope, and exploring their secrets with telescopes that bring increasing vistas of the heavens into his ken. Yet all the while he knows that deep within himself there is something more profound and more wonderful than all the stars of heaven, for he has been gifted with powers that link him to the Infinite.

Is it not noteworthy that scientists, using the methods of observation and analysis, have found themselves in complete agreement with the spiritual record of Genesis?

Here is a statement drawn up by fifteen notable men of science, including Robert A. Millikan, Michael Pupin, Henry Fairfield Osborn, and others: "It is a sublime conception of God which is furnished by science, and one wholly consonant with the highest ideals of religion, when it represents Him as revealing Himself through the inbreathing of life into its constituent matter, culminating in man with his spiritual nature and all his God-like powers." Surely this is an echo of the words of Genesis: "The Lord God formed man of the dust of the ground, and breathed into his nostrils the breath of life; and man became a living soul."

Years ago, while browsing through some old magazines, I came upon an incident quoted from an archeological journal. The story was told of certain excavators who had broken into an underground tomb. For one fleeting instant, on a ledge of rock, they saw the body of a beautiful maiden, dressed in grave's clothes. In a moment, because of the inrush of air, the body dissolved in a cloud of yellow dust. One of the explorers walked over to the ledge and brushed his hands along it, gathering into it all that had been the body of a human being—just one handful of dust.

Who could believe that this handful of dust had ever lived and loved, suffered and enjoyed, had stood out in the open night and looked up with wonderment to the heavens, lifting up hands of prayer to God? Just a handful of dust! Yes, but a handful of dust infused with the divine Spirit, permeated with the breath of God! It was the same spirit that dwelt in unlimited measure in Jesus Christ, who took upon him the form of a servant and was made in the likeness of man, who came to our earth to show us human life as God intended it to be lived, and to win rebellious man back to his loving heavenly Father.

The central aim of creation, according to Jesus, is the triumph of love. God is love. Love is not a solitary virtue. Love demands fellowship. Love is never perfected until it it shared. Even God had to share his love, and he revealed that love in the gift of his Son to the world.

The word "religion" is from *religare* and means "to bind back." So the chief end of man is not merely to be the eyes of the universe and to behold its beauty, or to be the mind of the universe and to work out its laws, but to be the heart of the universe, and to bind it back in loving response to the God who has created it. Only so is the mission of Christ fulfilled. Only then will war's wild clangor be heard no longer, and we shall see a new heaven and a new earth, wherein dwelleth righteousness.

The Faith That Redeems

And Pilate, willing to content the people, re-
leased Barabbas unto them, and delivered Jesus,
when he had scourged him, to be crucified.
—MARK 15:15

IT IS NINETEEN centuries since the long procession ascended
Calvary to crucify Jesus of Nazareth, but one cannot
read the story without feeling that there is an *eternal* element
in this drama, that the Crucifixion, while occurring in time,
also belongs to all the ages. The Bishop of London, Dr.
Ingram, stressed this fact. He says that it "stretches with
easy and terrible reach not only forward to the last moment
which shall pass on earth but back to the earliest dawn of
the foundation of the world."

So, too, one discovers in the Cross a *contemporary* significance. It is relevant to our own day. It touches the life
of every one of us. The men who drove Christ to the Cross
were not monsters of wickedness. They were simply a cross
section of humanity. It would not be difficult to find their
counterpart in the life of our time. Who were they? A
Roman Governor who sacrificed justice that he might remain in power; a disciple of Jesus who had become soured
by envy and greed; a reactionary ecclesiastic who used
fraud and lies to defend his own prejudices; a princely ruler
who cared more for the gratification of his passions than
that an innocent man was going to his doom. If we are
realistic, we shall recognize in the faces around the Cross

78

the features of modern people. Indeed, we may recognize our own!

The contemporary element in the Cross was brought home to me shortly after the First World War by an event that was altogether unforgettable. I was motoring in France with an American businessman whose brother had been killed in action while serving with our artillery unit. He said: "I want you to take me to every place where your battery was located. Especially I want to see the billets in which my brother slept and the cemetery where he and his comrades are laid away."

As we motored through northern France, we came to Neuve Chapelle. Our battery had been near there for a considerable period. At the entrance to the village we came face to face with the Wounded Christ. It was just a shrine like any one of the wayside shrines in many parts of France. But there was this difference: it bore a terribly mutilated Christ. The shell splinters and bullets had torn gaping holes in the head and face. Only the stump of the right leg remained. The left was blown off at the knee. The body was rent with shrapnel wounds and stained with poison gas. That shrine with its awful burden held us with a terrible fascination. Then the overwhelming thought came to me that this cross had been located in No Man's Land for the greater part of the war, and that our bullets and shrapnel, our shells and gas had wounded the Christ.

As he hung there looking out with sorrowful eyes over the landscape which still bore the marks of bitter conflict, he seemed to be passing judgment upon the whole world for its sins, and I recognized the contemporary element in the Crucifixion.

That Shrine at Neuve Chapelle is a parable of the way in which the Cross of Christ searches and judges and condemns us all.

You drove the nails in his white, white feet;
    I pierced each tender hand.
And we laughed as we lifted the cross on high—
    Too wise to understand.

You gave him the gall and vinegar;
    I thrust the lance in his side.
Yet they say it was years and years ago
    That the Saviour was crucified.[1]

It is especially significant that the Christian Church has singled out one man above all others as chiefly responsible for the death of Jesus. The Apostle's Creed says: "Suffered under Pontius Pilate." Yet Pilate is only the representative of a mighty host in our day as in Jesus' day—the morally indifferent people.

They had seen his matchless life. They had listened to his words such as never man spake. Their own hearts told them, "This Man's message is God's own truth." But they didn't care. They went their indifferent way regardless of the fate of Jesus. It was no concern of theirs. On the morning of the Crucifixion, two of them met at a street corner in Jerusalem and one said to the other: "I hear they are crucifying the Galilean today."

That was all! And with a shrug of their shoulders, they went their way. The crucifixion of Jesus was finally made possible by the people who didn't care. Pontius Pilate was their representative for, "willing to content the people . . . he delivered Jesus, when he had scourged him, to be crucified."

He knew what was right. He knew what he ought to do. A moment before he had declared that Jesus was innocent. Yet he delivered him into the hands of his cruel enemies. That was the easiest way. Any other course would have involved trouble, and Pilate did not believe in facing a conflict on a

[1] Edgar Daniel Kramer, "Good Friday." Used by permission.

moral issue. It was easier to sacrifice Jesus. And he had noticed that there wasn't a solitary voice lifted up in his defense in the judgment hall. Pilate had grown weary of the uneven conflict with the high priests. What was the life of one Galilean peasant in comparison with his own peace and safety? And so he proceeded to wash his hands!

Pontius Pilate is the exemplar of all those who, on a moral issue, choose the line of least resistance.

Shakespeare, in his tragedy *Richard II* makes the King say to his enemies:

> Nay, all of you that stand and look upon me
> Whilst that my wretchedness doth bait myself,
> Though some of you with Pilate wash your hands
> Showing an outward pity; yet you Pilates
> Have here deliver'd me to my sour cross,
> And water cannot wash away your sin.

Is not moral indifference a devastating sin of our own time? The most stubborn obstacle to a better world is not the outright enemies of God but the mass of people who do not care one way or another. Look at our own land. In recent years young men saw the disruption of all their plans, sacrificing in many instances remunerative employment, and went forth to the deserts of Africa or the jungles of the Orient to hazard their lives for freedom. At the same time, there were also men and women whose major endeavor was to gain what advantage they could for themselves out of a nation's agony.

The morally indifferent people do not care whether justice and righteousness will win or lose; whether the Church of Christ will live or die; whether this postwar world will usher in a new day for man or prove but another prelude to universal war.

It has been well said that, "Life is one long conflict between the motives of Jesus and the forces that drove Him to the Cross." And we are all taking sides.

Every time we choose a lower instead of higher course and yield to our baser selves, we are identifying ourselves with the enemies of Jesus. And when, in scorn of consequence, we bravely stand for the right we are aligning ourselves with him.

George Tyrrell of England, because of his battle for truth, was expelled from the Jesuit Order and practically excommunicated by the Roman Catholic Church. In the midst of the conflict he wrote: "Again and again I have been tempted to give up the struggle, but always the figure of that strange Man hanging on the Cross sends me back to my tasks again."

That Man on the Cross is worth living for, aye, he is worth dying for. And when the achievements and glories of man have crumbled into dust, his Cross will still stand "towering o'er the wrecks of time," the symbol of God's eternal victory.

The greatest miracle of the Cross is that even in the moment when it judges and condemns us, it also proclaims a message of hope, for it tells us of a God who "so loved the world, that he gave his only begotten Son, that whosoever believeth in him should not perish, but have everlasting life."

Recently a man was brought in to see me. I say "was brought in" because he was on the verge of desperation and was accompanied by a friend. He had earned distinction in the service of his nation, but had been utterly defeated within. There wasn't a thing that I could say to him that gave him encouragement. Invariably he replied: "There is no use—I am through. I am a beaten man and I know it. Death is the only way out."

There was nothing I could do for him, nothing—until I began to tell him about the Cross and of One who loved man enough to die for him, of One who believed in the redeemability of every human soul. When I finished that story, I saw hope light up his face with a glory greater than that of an Alpine sunrise.

But the One of whom we think this morning is no longer hanging on the Cross. He is no longer victim. He is victor. He is the crucified but risen Lord. He walks life's common way with us. Just when we think we are alone, we become aware of a Friend beside us. He knows how hard the battle has been, how often we have been defeated. His strong hand keeps us steady and we are not alone, for beside us is One, unseen to the eye of sense, whose form is like unto the Son of God.

> To this dear Cross the eyes of men are turning,
>   Today as in the ages lost to sight,
> And as for thee, O Christ, men's hearts are yearning—
>   As shipwrecked seamen yearn for morning light.

The Faith That Transforms

*And they were all amazed at the mighty power
of God.* —LUKE 9:43

ONE COLD WINTER morning, very near the beginning of my
ministry, I was urgently summoned to a General Hospital.
As I went to the emergency entrance I saw a box sleigh and
on a mattress in it a young boy was lying, his face as white
as death. Swiftly he was transferred to a stretcher and
taken to the operating room. Later, as the surgeon emerged,
the father of the boy rushed up to him and said: "Doctor,
can you help us? Can you save my son?" There was pain
in the doctor's eyes as he looked sadly at the father and
said: "I am terribly sorry; there is not a thing we can do."

That episode is indelibly engraved upon my mind, for
to me it is an epitome of man's helplessness in the face of
tragic human need.

Always this occurrence comes back to me as I read of
the happening at the foot of the Mount of Transfiguration.
While our Lord, with three of his disciples, was enwrapped
in the glory of Heaven, the remaining nine disciples stood
at the base of the mountain, in the valley, surrounded by the
scribes and Pharisees and a great crowd of people.

These religious leaders, discovering the disciples in the
absence of their Master, began to badger them with taunts
and questions.

At this juncture a distracted father arrived with his
stricken son. He pleaded with the disciples to cure him.
As they stood looking at the sick boy, they knew that their

84

Master had often healed maladies such as this. One after the other they stepped forth and tried to help him. They entreated, but they were not heard; they commanded, but they were not obeyed. One by one they tried, and one by one they failed. Still the boy writhed in torment, and every moment the crowd grew more hostile and more scornful.

Just at the height of the crisis, someone in the crowd shouted: "Look yonder, the Galilean is coming!" As the crowd turned in the direction indicated, they saw Jesus making his way down the mountainside.

With one accord the whole crowd surged toward him. Suddenly they stopped in bewilderment. They were thunderstruck. An awed silence fell upon them. They looked at Jesus in amazement. They had seen him before, but now there was something strangely different in his appearance.

For a clue to their astonishment, we must go back to the account of what happened on the holy Mountain. Luke says, "The fashion of his countenance was altered." In Moffatt's translation the meaning is much clearer: "The appearance of his face was altered."

He had been going through a time of dreadful testing as he faced the ordeal of the Cross. But now all the lines of care, of anxiety, and of tension had relaxed, and the glory and majesty of God was reflected in his face. Even the most thoughtless in the crowd sensed something of the afterglow of the Transfiguration.

When Moses came down from Mount Sinai where he had received the Law from God, it is recorded that the skin of Moses' face shone, and he "wist not that it shone." How much more true must this have been of the face of Jesus!

The awed silence was broken by a pitiful cry: "Master, I beseech thee look upon my son, for he is mine only child. I besought thy disciples to heal him and they could not. If thou canst do anything have compassion on us and help us."

Jesus turned his compassionate gaze upon the father, and replied: "If thou canst believe, all things are possible to him that believeth."

In a voice broken with sobs, the father answered: "Lord, I believe; help thou mine unbelief."

For a moment the Master stood looking down at the helpless child and then uttered a word of command that called forth divine energies beyond man's power either to compute or to understand. The stricken child was made whole.

What an unexpected climax was this! Just a few moments before, the disciples had stood baffled and defeated, surrounded by the jeering crowd. Now the multitude is hushed into silence by a demonstration of "the mighty power of God." What was it that so dramatically changed defeat into victory? Was it not this: *the Lord of the disciples came over the horizon and took his place in their midst.*

Two theories have been offered as to the manner in which the transformation of the world must be wrought. The first is that man can accomplish the task alone; his wisdom and his skill will legislate and engineer a new world into being.

A little over eighty years ago the Secularist League meeting in Europe published a manifesto declaring: "Science has made God unnecessary." Millions of people since that day have lived on this presumption. But we who have survived World War II have experienced the shock of a shattering disillusionment. The brutal logic of events has forever ended man's naive hope of inevitable human progress. Today we are the victims, not the masters, of these blind, materialistic forces we have unleashed, and everyone is afraid.

Science has made God unnecessary! Nay, say, rather, science without God is an abyss into which no thinking man dare direct his gaze.

In the second place, there are those who tell us that God alone will build his Kingdom on earth; that man must be

submissive and inactive; he must simply wait for the divine
fulfillment.

They assure us that all the efforts we make for world
betterment are doomed to frustration; that someday God
will flash forth with all-conquering power from heaven and
make a new world. The final truth is in neither of these
theories.

Ever since the day of Pentecost God has been teaching
his church that the Kingdom will come neither by man's
unaided effort nor by divine fiat, but through God and man
working in harmony. Man is the instrument or agent of
the divine power and the fulfiller of the divine will. Only
as our willful hearts are brought into accord with the purposes of the Eternal God will peace ever dawn upon this
broken and war-scarred world.

Have you ever noticed that pessimism, fear, and despair
are contagious? They pass through a crowd from person to
person like a charge of electricity.

It was so with the disciples of Jesus. They were unnerved
by the fierceness of the opposition. They hesitated, faltered,
and failed. They saw only the incredulous crowd—blank,
staring, unbelieving faces, and they were stampeded by fear.

Every morning in New York City hundreds of thousands
of persons tune in on their radios. What do they hear?
They learn of impending industrial conflicts; airplane dis-
asters; forest fires; hunger and want and misery around the
world; angry words spoken in the United Nations As-
sembly; hostility and hate, suspicions and fears; and over
all the dreadful threat of World War III, until the hearts
of men are filled with foreboding and fears, so that

> The native hue of resolution
> Is sicklied o'er with the pale cast of thought.

Depressed and bewildered, they carry their pessimism
out into the day until all society is plagued with fear.

They begin the day by tuning in on the feverish doings of man, but forget to tune in on God.

Let us remember that defeat and despair were changed for the disciples into resounding triumph when Christ came over the horizon and took his rightful place in their midst! The Christian Church, like the disciples of old, is all too often baffled and defeated, but once the Master appears and takes his place in the heart and center of the Church then power goes forth that makes the world stand in awe.

"If thou canst believe," said Jesus, "all things are possible to him that believeth." How remarkable that the divine power can be restrained and hindered by the unbelief of man! Says the Gospel record: "He could do there no mighty work because of their unbelief." Man's unbelief throws up a barrier against the operation of God's power because we are not automata, but children gifted with freedom of will. Only through loving and willing obedience can we serve our Maker.

God's mercy is like a boundless sea, but man has built retaining walls to confine it. The divine mercy beats endlessly against these barriers. When here and there a gate is flung wide open, the power of Almighty God flows through joyously and triumphantly on its mission of healing and redemption.

I know not what your special need is, but I know that there are hundreds of problems represented among those who read this message: some lives are weighted down with burdens heavier than they can bear; others are fretted with inner tensions and unresolved conflicts. A smiling face oftentimes conceals an aching heart. The unremitting struggle against base desires or the sense of futility and frustration rob life of its joy.

The day of victory will dawn for you the moment you see Christ come over the horizon and take his place in the very center of your life. Call upon Christ for help; fill your life with Christ, and there is no moral or spiritual problem that will remain unsolved.

What happens when Christ takes possession of a human life? Well, I witnessed an unmistakable answer to that question just seven years ago. A Sunday afternoon meeting was held on the grounds of a country estate in Florida. The speaker was one of the best-known Christians in the world, Sir Wilfred Grenfell.

We sat there enthralled, listening to his words, and looking into his sun-tanned, weather-beaten face. He told how even at the height of Labrador blizzards he journeyed with his dog team to the homes of the poor fishermen on errands of mercy. As he related his experiences, we knew that he brought to the suffering not only skillful hands, but also a loving heart.

Then he told of a day when from the shore they saw a fishing vessel with a distress signal flying. He put out in a boat, and found on the schooner an eighteen-year-old girl. She had shipped aboard as a cook. A few days earlier she had prematurely given birth to a baby, and was almost at the point of death.

Tenderly ministering to her, Dr. Grenfell saw that medical skill could offer no aid. Her life was gradually slipping away. He spoke to her gently of One who said: "Come unto me, all ye that labor and are heavy laden, and I will give you rest," and she found the peace that passeth all understanding.

Then he added: "We laid her tenderly away on a headland jutting out into the Atlantic, and from its summit one could see far across the restless waters. Over the grave I planted a rude wooden cross on which were carved the compassionate words of Jesus: 'Neither do I condemn thee.' "

As he talked, momentarily it seemed to me that Dr. Grenfell had faded from sight and in his place stood One whose form was like unto that of the Son of God.

What a world this would be if men and women would open their lives as Grenfell did to the inflowing power of Christ. Little wonder that he reminded people of the Master. Faith is energy; faith is force; faith is a creative influence that transforms men and women into Christlikeness.

This is our business. The Church exists exactly for this purpose. We are here to bring men and women into living touch with Jesus Christ. As we increasingly fulfill our mission, there will go forth the contagion, not of doubt and pessimism and fear, but of hope and faith and courage and confidence and love until all will sense the presence of the power of God.

Do you believe that this task is worth while? Then take your place in the ranks of Christian workers. Make your life count for God, and the day will come when the unthinking, heedless, churchless multitudes will turn their feet into the way of God's commandments and His Kingdom will come with a suddenness that will be the wonder of the world.

The Faith That Builds

*Put ye on the Lord Jesus Christ and make not
provision for the flesh to fulfill the lusts thereof.*
—ROM. 13:14

THE CHRISTIAN FAITH, as it is often presented today, lacks
heroic and adventurous qualities. It doesn't demand enough
of people. Everything is made too easy. This is because it
has conformed itself too much to our present-day civilization. Henry C. Link says that "all the material advantages
of our civilization conspire to make our lives easier and our
characters weaker."

There is no doubt that we have become soft and self-
indulgent in our outlook on religion. If it be true that
"character is the sum of all that we have struggled against,"
then we need not be surprised if in comparison with our
forefathers we moderns are lacking in moral fiber. There are
people in our midst who are incapacitated nervously mainly
because they lack constructive tasks to perform. They have
become casualties of ease and boredom.

Some twenty years ago the *Brave New World*, by
Aldous Huxley, was a best seller. It portrayed the kind of
life that still appeals to a great many people. It pictured the
world as science would make it: pain, struggle, discomfort,
effort, were all to be eliminated, and just to make assurance
doubly sure in case a little bit of irritation might creep in
there was always the drug "soma" which took the rough
edges off life.

Near the close of the story there is introduced a new

91

character, a savage who has come from the outer fringes of that anemic civilization. He meets the Controller of the world, and the Controller explains to him the kind of society that exists. Then he adds: "Just in case somebody might be overtaken by reverses or trouble, we have *soma* close at hand to give them a holiday from the troublesome facts." But, sad to say, when the holiday was over the troublesome facts were still there, staring them in the face, and they were even less capable of facing realities than they were before their journey into oblivion.

When the story of the brave new world had been told the heroic savage replied: "That is just like you, getting rid of everything unpleasant. . . . It is too easy. I don't want comfort; I want God. I want poetry; I want danger; I want freedom; I want goodness."

The one rebel against the brave new world is the only worthy character in the book.

If this type of civilization ever became an actuality, the race would sink below the level of the human plane, for the highest and noblest development man has achieved has come through conflict and adversity.

Some people still ask: "Why should God have created a world in which there is poverty and war and famine and human suffering on a colossal scale?" They fail to see that all the factors which make possible human happiness and achievement will, if misdirected, produce calamity and pain. We may have either good or evil, joy or misery, gain or loss, as we choose, because we have been created morally free, in the image of God. Conceivably God could have made a different kind of world. He could have created millions of automata instead of men and women. Then in some distant part of the universe he could have a vast, celestial switchboard, with innumerable buttons. The moment he pressed a button, an automaton would immediately carry out his will in perfect obedience. But automata could never become children of God, capable of holding communion with their heavenly Father and of proffering to him a willing and loving obedience.

Is there a human parent anywhere who would accept an automaton for a child? Love craves responsiveness, and the highest in man responds to God.

Omar Khayyam protests against our kind of world:

> Ah Love! could you and I with Him conspire
> To grasp this sorry Scheme of Things entire,
> Would not we shatter it to bits—and then
> Re-mold it nearer to the Heart's Desire!

His idea of a perfect world is a painless, effortless existence, under the shade of the grapevine, with a jug of wine and his love.

In man's noblest hours, however, he prefers the world as God has created it, a world of risks and adventure, with the thrill of battling hardships and the zest of conflict and victory.

There is great value in self-denial. We are all too self-indulgent. Any discipline we apply to ourselves will bring unmistakable gain if it is employed for the purpose of spiritual development. Self-denial should be channeled into a constructive undertaking, such as the feeding of the hungry peoples of liberated Europe.

Spiritual discipline, unlike military discipline, which is oftentimes very irksome, is not imposed from without; it emerges from within. It is self-imposed. It builds steadfast character and self-reliant personalities.

The New Testament says that "Discipline always seems, for the time, to be a thing of pain and not of joy; but those who are trained by it reap the fruit of it afterward in the peace of an upright life."

The best of all discipline is that which we apply to our inner life in molding character. We should endeavor to eliminate unchristian attitudes and tendencies by becoming less censorious in our judgments of other people and more exacting on ourselves; less demanding on the loved ones in our homes and more generous and thoughtful of them; more alert to the needs of other people and less preoccupied with our own. Here is a challenging task that will bring substantial spiritual gains.

Sometimes the psychologists help us greatly. Here are a few questions which one of them asks:

Do you lose your temper easily?

Do you get blue and sulk when things don't go your way?

Do you fuss about simple happenings?

Are you a bad loser?

Have you constructive work to do day by day?

Do you run away from difficulties?

Have you never practiced doing things you don't like to do?

That last question is most important. William James has often reminded us that character is disciplined and strengthened by our doing worth-while things that we would rather not do. Life is not an easy road for any of us, and to succeed we shall need the help of Christ.

Paul realizes this and points the way to self-conquest: "Put on the Lord Jesus Christ and make no provision for the flesh."

"Put on the Lord Jesus Christ." Let us examine some modern translations of this text even as we put a diamond under a magnifying glass and turn it round and round to see its different facets.

Moffatt renders it: "Put on the character of the Lord Jesus Christ."

Weymouth translates it: "Put on, as your armour, the Lord Jesus Christ."

Goodspeed says: "Clothe yourselves with the Lord Jesus Christ."

James Denney comments on the text: "The principle of

all such acts is the Spirit of Christ dwelling in us." That is
the root of the matter. Now, how may we receive his
Spirit? How shall we open our lives to his incoming?
Chiefly by a daily surrender to Christ's will for us; by daily
Bible reading, always continuing to read until we come
upon a verse that speaks to our own inner spiritual needs;
by daily prayer, whereby we wait upon God and say:
"Speak, Lord, for Thy servant heareth"; by regular church
attendance for the worship of him who has promised that
when we are met together in his name that he is in the midst
of us; by Bible study, such as the midweek service every
Wednesday night; by attendance at the special services.
All these means which I have enumerated will help us to
"put on the Lord Jesus Christ."

Our text is associated with one of the great men of history,
Augustine. As a youth he was full of licentiousness. Later
he met some noble Christians, and was filled with shame at
his own lack of self-control. It was at this stage of his career
that he prayed: "God, give me chastity, but not yet."

Tormented by the vast gulf between his ideals and his
conduct, he journeyed to Milan. Seated in the house with his
best friend, the young Roman Alypius, he talked of his
problems. The soul of Augustine was torn with bitter conflict. A sudden gust of tears drove him from the house into
the garden, and he flung himself on the grass, crying: "O,
God, how long! Tomorrow and tomorrow and tomorrow!"
Then he heard a voice saying: "Tolle lege," "take up and
read." Hurrying into the house, he took up the Epistle to
the Romans and began to read just where his eye lighted on
the page: "Not in rioting and drunkenness, not in chambering and wantonness, not in strife and envying, but put ye on
the Lord Jesus Christ, and make no provision for the flesh
to fulfill the lusts thereof."

He tells us of his emotions in that moment. "I neither
cared nor needed to read any further. At the close of the

sentence, as if a ray of certainty were poured into my heart
—the clouds of hesitation fled at once."

Williston Walker, the historian, adds: "From that moment he had peace of mind, and the sense of divine power
to overcome his sins which he had thus far sought in vain."

Later, when one of his former boon companions saw him
and called out: "Augustine, it is I," the man who became
one of the greatest leaders of the Christian Church replied:
"It is no longer I."

Each of you knows his own burden. Each of you knows
the secret problem of his life. Only God and you know
how hard the battle goes. I proclaim to you on the authority
of the living Word of God and on the basis of repeated
experiences of the divine power that there is no moral problem which Christ cannot solve.

"Put ye on the Lord Jesus Christ!"

Fill your life with Christ, think of him throughout the
hours of the day, think of him especially in times of temptation, and such strength as you have never known before
will be given to you.

> Every virtue we possess
> And every victory won
> And every thought of holiness
> Are His alone.

COURAGE TO OVERCOME

Courage for the Discouraged

For our high priest is not one who is incapable of sympathy with our weaknesses, but he has been tempted in every way just as we have without committing any sin. So let us come with courage to God's throne of grace to receive forgiveness and to find him responsive when we need his help.
—HEB. 4:15, 16 (Goodspeed)

MORE THAN A century ago Ralph Waldo Emerson delivered an address to the Divinity School at Harvard University. It created something of a sensation in the religious world. Not a little of what he said one hundred and eleven years ago is still applicable to the life of our time.

This is especially true of his remarks on the subject of preaching. He told the seminary students that the true preacher can be known by this, that he deals out to his people his life—life passed through the fire of thought. Then he added that he had once heard a preacher who sorely tempted him never to go to church again. The entire service, as well as the sermon, was divorced from life. One would never have surmised, said Emerson, that the preacher had ever lived at all; that he had ever laughed or wept; that he had been married or in love; that he had ever been cheated or chagrined; that his head had ever ached or his heart had throbbed; that he had lived or acted in the world.

Certainly the sage of Concord is right in this, that religion divorced from life becomes a cold, dead formalism. It has no message of hope for the worshiper who comes to the house of God while his thoughts are with a loved one in some sickroom; it has no word of consolation for those who have laid their dead away, and feel that their very heart has been left in the sepulcher; it has no word of guidance for those who are confused and bewildered on life's perplexing pathway; no word of counsel for those frustrated and disillusioned by the evils that have mastered their lives. Religion divorced from life leaves the worshiper defrauded and disconsolate.

Christian preaching at its best has always dealt with life— "life passed through the fire of thought." It would be difficult to find a more suitable illustration of preaching at its best than that afforded by Phillips Brooks. When at the height of his career in the Christian ministry, he said that the keynote of his preaching was life: "I have but one sermon and one text: 'I am come that they might have life, and that they might have it more abundantly.' " Brooks possessed the power of universal sympathy, of entering into the lives and problems of men and women so that the scholar and the unlettered, the rich and the poor, all claimed him as their own. He entered sympathetically into their trials and disappointments and successes, and offered healing power for the soreness of heart that was common to them all. One worshiper was heard to remark as he left Trinity Church in Boston after one of Brooks's sermons: "He makes me feel so strong."

A biographer says: "He walked with God; he conversed with Christ as his most intimate friend. He loved his earthly friends and enjoyed their companionship, but for none of them had he such attachment as for Christ."

"He conversed with Christ as his most intimate friend." That was the source of his power. That is the secret, not only of great preaching, as in the case of Brooks, but it is the secret of all great living: to walk and talk with Christ. The New Testament declares that Christ is not One who is incapable of sympathizing with our weaknesses, but was tempted in every way just as we are without committing any sin.

This divine Friend is full of sympathy for us, because he, too, fought on the battlefields of human life. He, too, tasted the bitterness of conflict; he, too, came to grips with hateful evil forces that sought his defeat and humiliation, but unfailingly he emerged a victor. Now, there are some Christian people who hesitate to believe that Christ was tempted. They forget that to rob him of his conflict is to rob him of his victory. He had to face not merely the temptation in the wilderness. Temptations assailed him throughout his life right to the foot of the Cross. And let it never be forgotten that he won through by using the same spiritual resources that are open to you and to me—the strength of his own character and the spiritual power that came to him from God in answer to prayer.

Jesus employed no unnatural means to gain the victory —no supernatural charms which are denied to us; no private miracle of his own. He fought the devil standing where we stand, and with the same weapons that are ready to our hands. Otherwise, his example would have little value for you and me. When a man is standing with his back to the wall, battling for his soul, he will despise the smooth counsel of one who has gained the victory through spiritual short cuts denied to others, and by special endowments that no one else can ever share. The advice to which we listen, and the encouragement which we receive is from him who battled through blood to victory. No, if Christ is to be my helper and my encourager he must needs have fought the battle on the same terms as I. That is exactly what the New Testament says: "He was tempted in all points as we are."

It is well to remind ourselves that temptation is not a sin. It is not a sin to discover that in some unguarded moment wretched and debasing thoughts have entered your minds. It is not a sin to feel the downward pull of the lower self. It is not a sin to be tempted to take the lower course rather

than the higher. It is only a sin when we yield to baseness.
It is only a sin when we give a loose rein to evil impulses.
It is only a sin when we disobey that "great beacon light"
that God has placed within us. Jesus was in truth without
sin, but he was not without temptation. In the agony of his
travail in Gethsemane his sweat was as great drops of blood
falling to the ground.

While we remember that it is no sin to be tempted, let us
not forget that daily resistance builds up strength of character which will make the next victory easier until
we become self-mastered because we are Christ-mastered. It
is this self-identification of Jesus with sinful men and women,
the fact that he entered into our human lot, that he shared
our battles, which makes him the supreme Friend of man.
He understands. He tasted the sweetness and the bitterness
of life. He shared every kind of human experience. He
scaled the heights and he plumbed the nethermost depths.
So he is a Friend in every circumstance of joy or pain.

The New Testament speaks often of the deep sympathy
of Jesus. Listen to these expressive words: "When he saw
the multitude he was moved with compassion on them because they fainted and were scattered abroad as sheep having
no shepherd." In the presence of human misery, the compassion of our Lord was powerfully manifested. His out-
reaching sympathy won to him Simon Peter and his fishermen friends; Zaccheus, the dishonest tax gatherer of Jericho;
Mary Magdalene, in the sevenfold grip of evil forces; blind
Bartimeus by the wayside, and a host of others who were
lifted up and redeemed by his friendship. But nowhere else
does the spirit of our Lord shine forth with such undimmed
splendor as in the case of the woman taken in adultery. The
scribes and the Pharisees brought her before him as he sat
teaching in the Temple. One of the craftiest of the lot
stepped forward and in a smooth, unctuous voice said:
"Master, Moses in the law says that a woman like this should
be stoned, but what sayest thou?"

These sanctimonious religionists were straining at the leash like hellhounds ready to leap upon their prey. It was a crafty snare which they prepared for Jesus. If he said: "I am opposed to this stern moral code of the long-ago," immediately they would have raised the cry of "blasphemy" and called for his arrest. If he sanctioned this terrible law, he would have alienated the common people who heard him so gladly. In modern parlance, they felt that they had "put Jesus on the spot," that he was on the horns of a dilemma, that there was no escape for him.

"Certainly," they said, "he will acquit the woman, for is not Mary Magdalene among his followers?" But Jesus made no reply. Instead of turning upon them as was his wont the scrutiny of his deep, searching eyes, he stooped down and with his finger began to write on the ground. They thought that at last they had him in their power, that he was bewildered by the problem, so they began to urge him: "What are you going to do? What do you say? What is your verdict in this matter?"

Why did Jesus stoop over and write on the ground? This is the only occasion on which he is ever reported to have written a word. What was his purpose? Sir John Seeley, in his famous essay "Ecce Homo" writes: "He was seized with an intolerable sense of shame. He could not meet the eyes of the crowd, or of the accusers, and perhaps at that moment least of all of the woman." This suggestion reverently offered by a scholar may be useful as an interpretation of the incident, but I doubt very much if it accords with the facts. As I read once again John's record of this incident, an explanation flashed into my mind which I believe is very close to the truth. Jesus was undoubtedly shocked by the heartlessness of these men who would use this poor woman as a pawn for the purpose of defeating and humiliating him, but it was not a sense of shame that made him stoop down and write on the ground. I believe that he was seizing a moment for prayer. Overwhelmed by this revelation of the

appalling sinfulness and cruelty of the human heart, he
sought a brief interlude for communion with his heavenly
Father. If he wrote any actual words on the ground, I think
they would be these: "Father, forgive them, for they know
not what they do."

As they continued to goad him, Jesus lifted himself up
and uttered one divinely inspired sentence which started
these men and left them utterly confused: "He that is without sin among you let him first cast a stone at her." Then
once again he bent down and wrote on the ground. That
one sentence was like the thrust of a rapier into the hearts
of the woman's accusers. One by one, beginning with the
eldest, these scribes and Pharisees sneaked out of his presence
like whipped curs, their heads hanging low and their cheeks
flushed with shame. When they had all gone, Jesus lifted
himself up once again and saw only the woman standing
there. He said: "Woman, where are thine accusers? Has
none condemned thee?"

Without looking up, she answered in a low voice: "No
man, Lord," and waited for judgment and bitter condemnation. But no word of blame fell from the lips of Jesus. His
penetrating glance had read the secret of a contrite and
penitent heart. He would not "break the bruised reed or
quench the smouldering flax." "Neither do I condemn thee,"
he said. "Go and sin no more."

Says David Smith: "Her condemnation was all the concern of the Pharisees; her salvation was all the concern of
Jesus."

> Down in the human heart, crushed by the Tempter,
>   Feelings lie buried that grace can restore;
> Touched by a loving hand, wakened by kindness,
>   Chords that are broken will vibrate once more.

Now perhaps you can better understand the significance
of one of the truly great passages of the New Testament:

We have not an high priest, which cannot be touched with the feeling of our infirmities; but was in all points tempted like as we are, yet without sin. . . . Let us therefore come boldly unto the throne of grace that we may obtain mercy and find grace to help in time of need."

Why, then should we let discouragements overcome us? Why should we be morally defeated? Why should we be satisfied with less than our best? Our great Advocate, Jesus Christ, stands ready to pour into our souls divine, victorious power that will make us more than conquerors through him who loved us. Remember he is your friend. He is not against you; he is for you; he is not condemning you for the failures of the past. He knows how fierce the battle has been; how easy it is to become disheartened. He walked life's hard road, and drank to its dregs the bitter cup. "In the world," he says, "ye shall have tribulation, but be of good cheer, for I have overcome the world."

Keep your eyes on the great Captain of your salvation, who never lost a battle. His spirit will make you believe in yourself, will call forth everything that is splendid within you. His strong arm is near to help, his brave eyes will keep you steadfast. With him beside you, you cannot fail.

Strength Out of Weakness

For when I am weak, then am I strong.
—II Cor. 12:10

When Sir Charles Darwin was engaged in his famous voyages in many parts of the world, always the keen eyes of the naturalist saw extraordinary things where other people saw only the commonplace.

On one occasion, while sailing in the Pacific Ocean along the coast of South America, his attention was attracted by an unusual type of seaweed. Leaning over the side of the ship he studied it intently, and then obtained some specimens. This weed, floating on the waves, was tossed about incessantly by wind and tide, and sometimes was flung violently against the precipitous walls of rock along the coast. Still it lived on while other forms of animal and vegetable life perished, and even the flinty rocks were ground to powder.

Impressed by these facts, Darwin took out his notebook and made this entry: "I know of few things more surprising than to see this plant growing and flourishing amid those great breakers of the western ocean which no mass of rock, be it ever so hard, can long resist." The secret of this plant's endurance was its suppleness, its flexibility, its inner strength and toughness. If that little seaweed had been gifted with speech, it could have truthfully said: "When I am weak, then am I strong."

Now this, of course, is a paradox. Webster defines a paradox: "An assertion seemingly contradictory or opposed to common sense but that yet may be true in fact." Robert Browning illustrates this figure of speech:

> For thence a paradox
> Which comforts while it mocks
> Shall life succeed in that it seems to fail.

Similarly, the Apostle Paul wrote: "When I am weak, then am I strong." Now, the circumstances that drew from the Apostle this paradox is worthy of our attention and study. He had become afflicted with what he called "a thorn in the flesh."

Many and varied have been the guesses of New Testament scholars respecting this affliction. Some think that it may have been defective eyesight; others, a recurrent form of malaria, or of *tic douloureux*, or even epileptic seizures. But all these conjectures are vain and time-wasting. The identity of this obscure malady will probably never be discovered. We know, however, that it caused the Apostle great humiliation, and, in all likelihood, severe pain. We may be confident that it was a physical and not a spiritual malady. How can we be so sure of this? Well, Paul would never have ceased praying for deliverance from it had it been a spiritual weakness. On three separate occasions the Apostle besought the Lord that he might be freed from this evil thing, but the thorn in the flesh remained. This fact might well be pondered by those who declare that unfailingly God will free human beings from every physical ill if only they have faith.

Let it be remembered, however, that the Apostle's prayer did not go unanswered. Instead of the physical healing for which he had prayed, God gave him a mighty accession of spiritual power. The Eternal said to him: "My grace is sufficient for thee, for my strength is made perfect in weakness." The malady remained, but it no longer mattered. It was submerged; it was swallowed up; it was completely vanquished by the divine, victorious power released in the Apostle's life! Now exultingly he can say: "Therefore, I take pleasure in weaknesses and insults, in hardships, in persecutions, in difficulties, when they are endured for Christ's sake, for when I am weak then am I strong." (II Cor. 12:10, Moffatt.)

The spiritual power which now welled up in his life gave him the victory, not only over the malady that harassed him, but over all the hardships and oppositions that beset his pathway. It was victory all along the line. He asked for a physical healing, and instead God gave him spiritual power that vitalized every area of his life. "When I am weak, then am I strong." A profound spiritual principle is revealed in our text: that divine power cannot be released in the life of any man until he is prepared to acknowledge his own powerlessness. "My grace is sufficient for thee," came the word of God to Paul, "for my strength is perfected in weakness." Moffatt translates it: "It is in weakness that my power is fully felt."

Spiritual principles do not appear in splendid isolation in only one segment of the Bible; they run like a golden thread throughout the Old and the New Testaments. When Zerubbabel, the servant of the Lord, had become alarmed because the forces at his disposal were insufficient for the tasks that awaited him, the word of God came to him saying: "Not by might nor by power, but by my Spirit saith the Lord of hosts."

Centuries earlier God called upon Gideon to deliver his people. To him was given one of the strangest commands ever presented to the leader of an army. God told him to prepare for victory by reducing the number of his forces. Consequently, Gideon offered a discharge to every man who was fearful or afraid. Twenty thousand of his soldiers went home. Two-thirds of the army melted away. Then he applied a second test to determine the alertness and the capacity for self-denial among the remaining ten thousand.

On the completion of this test, only three hundred warriors were left. Yet with this little handful of fighting men, and in complete dependence on God, Gideon won a resounding victory. He could well have uttered the words penned by Paul, "When I am weak, then am I strong."

In his first Epistle to the Corinthians Paul wrote these penetrating and unforgettable words: "God hath chosen the foolish things of the world to confound the wise; and God hath chosen the weak things of the world to confound the mighty; and the base things of the world and the things which are despised hath God chosen, yea, and things which are not, to bring to naught the things that are, that no flesh should glory in his presence."

Here surely is a lesson that the Christian Church in America would do well to learn. We are constantly tempted to believe that the effectiveness of the Church in any age is determined by the number of its adherents and the magnitude of its financial resources. Yet this is contrary to the teaching of the New Testament. The resourcefulness of the Church is not determined by any of these temporal assets, but only by the measure in which she utilizes the limitless power of her Lord. I venture to assert that the Apostolic Church of the first century, deficient in numbers, constantly persecuted, lacking in material riches, yet exercised a mightier spiritual influence than our American Christianity, Roman Catholic and Protestant combined, with all its prestige and power.

Periodically, we do well to search our hearts and to ask ourselves penetrating questions which test our effectiveness as Christians. First: Does my life day by day witness to the power of the gospel of Christ? Second: Does my faith in Christ affect the quality of my daily living, so that there adheres to it a nobility and moral strength? Third: Is there anything in my life that reminds men and women of the Master to whom I have pledged my allegiance? Fourth: Is there any discernible difference at all in my life as con-

trasted with the lives of those who have never acknowledged
Him? What answer can I truthfully make to Jesus' question: "What do ye more than others?" Fifth: Do I manifest
in the midst of this fevered generation a serenity of spirit
which reveals that the peace of God is dwelling in my heart?

These are reasonable questions for any Christian to ask
himself, and if we have to reply in the negative (and I fear
that many of us must indict ourselves with failure), then but
one prayer is fitting: "God be merciful to me, a sinner."
This prayer uttered with sincerity will bring to each of us
a profound spiritual blessing. Only as we humble ourselves,
acknowledging our deficiencies and allowing the power of
God to sweep through us, are we of use in the service of
his blessed Kingdom. "God be merciful to me, a sinner."
God comes to us in power when we make this prayer our
own, and he says: "My grace is sufficient for you; my
strength is perfected in your weakness."

The reason most of us fail is that we have overmuch trust
in our own resources. Pride is the source of many a man
and woman's downfall. We are confident of our self-suf-
ficiency. It is hard for us to admit our utter dependence on
God. Pride says: "No, you can depend on yourself." It is
hard to say: "Of myself I am certain to fail. Grant me thy
all-sufficient grace that in my weakness thy strength may
be made perfect."

A few years ago a layman appeared before the New York
State Medical Association's annual meeting and delivered a
memorable address. He was speaking at the request of the
officers of this association and took as his topic "Alcoholics
Anonymous." He was one of the founders of that organization.

The doctors listened with great interest as he outlined
the principles under which Alcoholics Anonymous operates.
Especially important are the first three of the "twelve steps"
in this organization. They are these:

First: We admitted we were powerless over alcohol; that

our lives had become unmanageable. Second: We came to believe that a Power greater than ourselves could restore us to sanity. Third: We made a decision to turn our wills and our lives over to God as we understand him. The speaker continued: "If the spiritual content of the twelve steps is actively denied, there is seldom ever any success in the treatment. We stress the spiritual simply because thousands of us have found that we cannot get along without it."

The reason for the success of Alcoholics Anonymous is the exaltation of the spiritual, the frank and complete admission of defeat and failure and inability to win out by unaided human efforts, and dependence on the power of God to bring its adherents through to self-conquest. It is a remarkable fact that the founders of Alcoholics Anonymous, desperately seeking for a remedy for the scourge of alcoholism, stumbled upon what is very near to the heart of the Christian gospel in its power to bring victory out of defeat.

William James, years before, wrote: "The whole development of Christianity on its inwardness consists in little more than greater and greater emphasis on the crisis of surrender." "Surrender" is the vital word. "Surrender" is one of the most meaningful terms in the Christian vocabulary. It denotes the moment when the penitent sincerely prays: "O God, I have nothing to offer thee of merit. I have failed in the past and shall continue to fail except thy hand be stretched forth to save. Let thy power be manifested in me."

One of the most notable interviews I have had in the last twelve months was the case of a man who found himself facing the greatest opportunity of his career. Should he not succeed, his failure would be spectacular and irretrievable. There was no apparent reason why he should fail. I said that there was no "apparent" reason. Deep down in his heart, however, this man knew that success was impossible, not because he lacked ability, but an inner weakness made him a lion shorn of his strength. Some day all men would know his dreadful secret. In desperation he sought help. Like a great light breaking upon his darkness came the word of God. "My grace is sufficient for thee, for my strength is made perfect in weakness." Day by day rejoicing in a strength greater than his own, he would say: "When I am weak, then am I strong." What had been an appalling weakness in his life now became the point of firmest resistance. This is the oft-repeated miracle of the grace of God. Where we are weak, he makes us strong.

Are you among those destined to receive such a blessing? Well, this will mean surrender and self-mastery through Christ-mastery.

Make me a captive, Lord,
And then I shall be free,
Force me to render up my sword,
And I shall conqueror be.

Healing the Hurts of Life

*To be carnally minded is death, but to be
spiritually minded is life and peace.* —Rom. 8:6

Mark twain once said: "If I were a heathen, I would erect
a statue to energy and fall down and worship it."

Well, Mark Twain didn't need to erect that statue because statues to energy are erected all across our nation.
Indeed, it would be difficult to find any more fitting symbol
of our national life than a statue to energy.

Think of the adjectives that are most popular today as we
describe our achievements: dynamic; aggressive; vigorous;
powerful. We are a people who worship energy! It is not
accidental that we should be the first in history to discover
the mightiest force known to man, atomic energy.

But there are other words of vital importance in human
parlance aside from those that I have enumerated: poise;
balance; serenity; steadfastness; tranquility; peace. These are
qualities absolutely indispensable to any well-ordered civilization or any well-organized life.

One of the clearest thinkers of our time has declared that
man's life is built on the same principle as a Gothic cathedral,
with balanced thrusts. Every new arch must be braced with
new foundations. In a cathedral such as Notre Dame in
Paris we see many flying buttresses. As the nave of a church
is enlarged the thrust from without must meet the push
from within. So in the life of a people the more extensive
our material achievements become the deeper and stronger
must be our moral and spiritual foundations.

Paul said: "To be carnally minded is death, but to be spiritually minded is life and peace."

What does he mean by "carnally minded"? The carnal mind is one whose spiritual faculties are dominated and enslaved by the material and the physical. In a civilization the carnal mind is dominant when material achievements outstrip the moral and spiritual. Now, is not that exactly the state of our modern world, and is it not from this situation that most of our stubborn problems emerge? All too much we have become a materially minded people. We concentrate our thoughts on things; consequently, we are in the midst of widespread nervous tension and dispeace.

For instance, in New York City, one in every eighteen persons has received or is now receiving psychiatric treatment. One in every eighteen!

A balanced life for the individual, as for a people, can be achieved only as we cease to fasten our thoughts constantly on external things and find an opportunity for meditation and the cultivation of that inner serenity and peace of which we stand in desperate need.

The great Marshal Foch said to a friend: "One of the worst features of our present-day civilization is that one never has time to meditate."

The Surgeon-General of the United States a few months ago announced to the people of this nation that heart disease is now far and away the major cause of death. Then he proceeded to enumerate the factors which have precipitated this condition, and foremost he places hypertension induced by our mode of living.

These facts stressed by Dr. Parran were dramatically brought home to a group of American businessmen a little time ago. The Heart Association, a medical association in the city of Chicago, invited eighty-five top-flight executives to a meeting. It was held in the Chicago Union League Club.

The doctors placed in front of the eighty-five men four glass containers in each of which was a human heart. The first heart was normal; the second heart was swollen, ballooned up to almost twice its normal size. They announced that this was the heart of a hot-tempered newspaper executive who died instantly while arguing with one of his assistants. The third heart belonged to a business executive who lived under constant tension and refused to relax or to slow down when advised to do so by his physician. He died while comparatively a young man. The fourth heart belonged to a businessman who suffered a heart attack at the age of sixty-five. He then commenced to learn how to live. He relaxed and began to enjoy life, and died peacefully at the age of eighty.

I am sure that it was a thoughtful group of men who went back to their offices that day.

The emotional factors which are most frequently the cause of inner tension are fears, anxieties, anger, jealousies, resentments, worries, and hate. The sovereign remedy of them all is faith, for "to be spiritually minded is life and peace."

On several occasions recently at the 5:30 rush hour, I have ridden up an escalator in a New York subway station. It happens to run parallel with another escalator that descends. I found myself looking into the faces of some seventy to one hundred persons who had just completed their day's work and were on their way home. It was impressive to note how tired most of them looked. There was strain and tension in many faces, with evidence of nervous exhaustion and irritability.

I could not help reflecting that on Sunday morning tens of thousands of people similarly situated will feed their souls on the Sunday morning papers and the radio—the same diet as on the other six days of the week. They will read and hear of conflicts and tensions and suspicions and hates and violence, with recurrent appeals to purchase this or that commodity. They expose themselves constantly to the impact of the temporal. The material crowds in upon them until their little souls are shriveled up and wither away and finally die.

Paul says in effect: "To be carnally minded is the road that leads to dissolution and death."

Senancour, the French writer, exhorts: "Let us keep our silent sanctuaries; for in them the eternal perspectives are revealed." Isn't that our basic need today, to keep ever a vision of "the eternal perspectives," and to know that we are not constantly "cabin'd, cribb'd, and confin'd" by material things, the dust that returns again to the dust? Rather shall we have the liberating knowledge that no matter how difficult life may be for each one of us, there are windows that open to the Infinite, and above and around and beneath us are the inexhaustible spiritual resources of the eternal God.

This is what Paul means when he speaks of being "spiritually minded," and it is the way of life and peace. So let us keep our "silent sanctuaries" at the beginning of each day with God and his Word. At intervals throughout the day even in the midst of the crowd, and when by thronging duties pressed, let us now and then turn aside for a brief moment and seek the face of our heavenly Father.

The saintly Bernard of Clairvaux has written: "Wherever thou shalt be pray secretly within thyself. If thou shalt be far from a house of prayer give not thyself trouble to seek for one; for thou art thyself a sanctuary designed by God for prayer."

"Thou art thyself a sanctuary designed by God for prayer." When you find the pressure of life in the midst of the busy day getting a little bit too much for you, close your eyes and commune with God, and spiritual reinforcement will come flooding into your soul, and you will know the peace of those who walk with him.

Another source of spiritual strength and healing is to be found in the services of the house of God. While it is true that we ourselves are sanctuaries designed by God for prayer, it is easier to become aware of his presence in those places where he has recorded his name, sanctuaries made sacred by the prayers of the saints.

Much will depend upon your own spiritual preparedness. If you come to a Sunday morning service with no greater thoughtfulness than you give to attending a movie house, barrenness of soul is likely to result.

Come in the spirit of expectancy. Believe that you will receive a blessing, and you will not be disappointed. Unite your prayers with those of an ever-increasing number of persons who set apart a brief period of each day for communion with God. Then on Sunday morning the power of the Lord will be mightily manifested.

Six weeks ago a woman came to New York from an upstate city. She said to her family: "I will return when I have found the answer to my problem." When she was here three weeks, she began to realize that she had been trying to run away from herself. Of course it was true that life had hurt her badly, but she had been striking back and had hurt others. There was hostility and constant tension in her home.

Then one Sunday morning, for the first time, she came to church. Later she said: "Strangely enough, the moment I entered I felt an atmosphere of quietness and peace, and as the service progressed that feeling deepened. The minister spoke of an occasion when he had heard Dr. Grenfell tell of his work in Labrador, and said that as the physician was speaking his face was so transfigured with the love of Christ that for a moment he seemed to have vanished and in his place stood One "whose form was like unto that of the Son of God."

"In that instant," said the woman, "I felt that Christ himself was present in the congregation, moving through our midst, touching men and women one by one and saying 'Peace be unto you.' I felt that his hands had been laid in benediction upon me. Then I knew that my problem had been solved, and that I would take back to my home the answer that I had found."

One would almost think that Henry van Dyke's poem had been written for this woman:

> With eager heart and will on fire,
> I sought to win my great desire.
> "Peace shall be mine," I said, but life
> Grew bitter in the endless strife.
>
> My soul was weary, and my pride
> Was wounded deep. To heaven I cried
> "God give me peace, or I must die."
> The dumb stars glittered no reply.
>
> Broken at last I bowed my head
> Forgetting all myself and said:
> "Whatever comes, His will be done."
> And in that moment peace was won.[1]

As Dante expressed it beautifully "In His will is our peace." Come, then, with this storm-tossed, harassed, stressful life of yours and bring it into the presence of the Great Physician. He is saying: "Come unto me all ye that labor and are heavy laden, and I will give you rest."

As you kneel in his presence, he will lay his hands upon you, saying: "Peace be unto you," and you will experience "the peace of God that passeth all understanding."

---

[1] Reprinted from *The Poems of Henry van Dyke.* Copyright 1911 by Charles Scribner's Sons, 1939 by Tertius van Dyke. Used by permission of the publishers.

Prayer--A Cosmic Power

Peter therefore was kept in prison: but prayer
was made without ceasing of the church unto God
for him.
—ACTS 12:5

IN THE YEAR 1876 a group of men stood round in a laboratory. They were watching experiments conducted by a young man twenty-nine years of age. He had before him a glass bulb, wire, and electric batteries. Turning to his companions, he said: "Put out those lights," indicating rows of candles and kerosene lamps. When the lights were extinguished, he said: "I am going to pull a switch, and when I do, you will see the first incandescent electric light ever devised by man."

The switch was pulled. There was an instantaneous flash of light, which was swallowed up immediately in darkness. A groan of disappointment came from the men standing round. When the candles were relighted, the young man turned to the group and said: "I'm sorry. I have a long way yet to go. The trouble is that the filament which I used had not sufficient strength to withstand the heat of the electric current. It was immediately consumed."

Little did he realize that three years of experimentation would pass and forty thousand dollars would have to be spent before that wonderful day when a loop of carbonized cotton thread would remain aglow in a vacuum for forty hours. Then he knew that the problem was solved.

The youth who conducted these experiments was Thomas A. Edison. What was it that kept him steadfast in the face of all these repeated discouragements? It was the knowledge that only his equipment had failed. He had abounding faith in the force with which he was dealing. The cosmic power known as electricity would not fail. Indeed, he had watched its operation on many a summer night as the forked lightning leaped from the black bosom of the sky, turning the Stygian darkness into blazing, blinding light. He knew that it could be counted upon. Electricity had not failed. Only the man who had sought to harness it had been temporarily frustrated.

This is an analogy of prayer. I know that prayer is not a vital and meaningful force in the lives of many people. It has become a mechanical routine from which little is expected and not very much is received.

Let it be remembered that this is a human failure. Prayer has not failed. It, too, is a dependable cosmic power.

It is a salutary corrective to turn from our modern skepticism and indifference with regard to prayer to the glowing faith of the early Church. The Book of the Acts tells of an hour of grave peril for first-century Christians. Herod Agrippa the First, the grandson of Herod the Great, stretched forth his hand to persecute the Church. He slew James, the brother of John, with the sword. These brothers were known as Boanerges, the Sons of Thunder. It may well be that James's passion for righteousness marked him out for destruction. Seeing that his action had rejoiced the enemies of the Christian faith, Herod reached out his hand and laid hold of one of the leaders of the little community, Simon Peter, and put him in prison.

The Jewish king had a vivid recollection of two previous occasions when this man Peter had escaped from prison. This time he would take no chances. To make assurance doubly sure, he placed the Apostle in charge of four quaterions of soldiers. Sixteen men, therefore, guarded him, four at a time, who remained on duty for three hours until relieved by another quaterion.

On the night of the betrayal Peter had said to his Master: "Lord, I will follow thee to prison and to death." Now it looks as though his words were prophetic. He is already in prison. On the morrow he will be brought forth for a mock trial followed in all likelihood by a cruel death.

In this hour of black foreboding, what could the little band of disciples do? Their friend was in the hands of King Herod. A powerful soldier guard and the grim walls of a prison with its staunch iron gates all stood in the way of his release. What did the Christians do? They could have conspired to find some way of effecting Peter's escape despite the seeming hopelessness of the situation. But instead of plotting they prayed. "Peter, therefore, was kept in prison, but prayer was made without ceasing of the church, unto God, for him."

These people believed in the value of intercession. They were convinced that in some wondrous way, beyond their understanding, prayer could reach behind the walls and bars of Herod's prison and touch with quickening power the life of Peter.

That is exactly what happened. The first evidence of an answer to their prayer was the fact that Peter slept. He lay between two Roman soldiers to whom he was fastened with chains, yet he slept soundly. He continued to sleep despite the fact that he knew that on the morrow he would be tried and in all probability sentenced to death.

Now I am fully aware that condemned felons, hardened in crime, knowing that there is no escape for them, have slept soundly on the night before their execution. That, however, is the grim resignation of despair. There was no slightest hint of this in the trustful sleep of Simon Peter. What an experience it must have been for those two soldiers who were his guards! In all probability they were pagan mercenaries. They didn't believe in God. In wonderment they watched the Apostle kneel in prayer before composing himself for sleep. They heard him remember his

Christian brethren in Jerusalem, commending them to the care of the heavenly Father. He also prayed for the soldiers who guarded him.

But there was no sleep for the little band of Christians in Jerusalem. All night long they continued in prayer while Peter slept as peacefully as did his Master amidst the storm on the Sea of Galilee when the raging waves threatened to engulf the little fishing boat and its crew. He slept as a little child sleeps in the security of its mother's arms. So always the power of God reaches out in response to our prayers and touches the lives of those for whom we intercede.

We may be quite sure that the other disciples meeting in prayer requested something more than that Peter might be kept steadfast in the hour of trial and granted unbroken rest. I am confident that they prayed also for his release, if God so willed. While Peter never manifested the statesmanlike leadership of Paul, yet his rugged courage was a great encouragement to his brethren. They needed his help. Luke, the physician, who is believed to be the author of the Acts, records the amazing story of the deliverance of Peter from prison and his restoration to his brethren.

A university student came to me to discuss this incident, which he had come upon in his study of religion. "That whole business," he said, "belongs to the realm of miracle. I can't understand these happenings, and therefore my intelligence compels me to dismiss them. How could that prison gate open of its own accord?"

I asked him if he had ever seen the iron gates that open of themselves in the Pennsylvania Station, New York.

"Oh, that is different," he said, "that I can accept because I understand it. We have covered that in our physics course at college."

"Would you mind explaining to me," I said, "exactly how these gates open?"

He launched into an elaborate explanation of photosensitized plates coated with metallic oxide. "The beam of light," he continued, "falls on these plates and the electrons on their surface are energized by the light. They actually borrow their power from the ray of light that strikes them. When the beam of light is broken, a change in voltage occurs, and a mechanism is activated which opens the gate."

"That is fine so far as it goes," I suggested, "but in your explanation you have been talking about electricity. Can you explain the nature of this force that operates in the opening of these iron gates?"

"I am sure I could if I knew enough physics," he said.

It happened that at the moment I had in a portfolio on my desk letters from four well-known scientists. All four said that science has no acceptable explanation of either matter or electricity. One of these physicists, who heads his department in a great American university, added that on one occasion a professor of physcis suddenly turned to an inattentive student and said: "Now, tell me, what is electricity?"

The student hesitated a moment and said: "I am very sorry, sir. I knew, but I have forgotten."

"What a tragedy," said the professor. "There sits the one man in the world who has ever known what electricity is, and he has forgotten."

When I showed this correspondence to the student sitting before me, he said: "Well, it looks as though I must accept some things that I can't understand, even in physics."

Many people will immediately concede that man, the creature, is constantly employing laws of the universe beyond his understanding for the accomplishment of his purposes, and yet they will deny that the Creator who fashioned these laws can use them to work his divine will.

The poet Cowper sees God constantly at work. He writes:

> There lives and works
> A Soul in all things and that Soul is God.

The Lord of all himself through all diffused
Sustains and is the life of all that lives.
Nature is but the name for an effect
Whose cause is God.

We are altogether too hesitant in utilizing the cosmic power released through prayer. Even medical scientists are reminding us of this, for Alexis Carrel has written: "The influence of prayer on the human mind and body is as demonstrable as that of secreting glands."

What the scientist says has been repeatedly vindicated as the pastor kneels in prayer by the bedside of a parishioner whom he commends to the healing power of God.

Medical science may have despaired of saving the patient, but the quiet, even-toned words of the minister quoting a well-loved passage from the Bible has had a strange and unlooked-for effect. The patient's will to live is strengthened. The hope of recovery reasserts itself. In response to the spiritual therapy of Scripture and prayer, healing forces of unpredictable power are at work, lifting this life from the very gates of death.

The physician of one of my parishioners telephoned me to say that his patient was not likely to pull through. It was his fourth operation in two years, and he had become utterly discouraged. The pain and weakness had been too much for him and the fight was out of him.

"If you visit him at all," said the physician, "please stay only a few minutes, as my patient is terribly weak. He no longer takes any interest in what is happening around him."

The next morning at nine o'clock the nurse ushered me into the sickroom and promptly left. The patient had failed almost beyond recognition. Taking his hand, I said: "Your doctor has told me that the way is now clear for your complete recovery. I am sure that God means you to get well. Remember the words of Jesus: 'Have faith in God.' At this very moment his healing power is flowing into your body. Have faith in God. Have faith in God."

When I left the sickroom after a visit that lasted only one minute, I thought I detected a slight change in my parishioner's eyes—a tiny light that indicated interest and perhaps a glimmer of hope.

Physician, nurse, and patient all testify that the period of convalescence really began that morning. Four months later my parishioner said to me: "Somehow those words 'Have faith in God' anchored me to this life when I seemed to be floating somewhere between heaven and earth. It was a strange and unforgettable experience."

Even more important is the power of prayer to keep well people healthy and sane, and in an untroubled frame of mind. It resolves the dark riddles of hidden fears and builds resolute and healthy-minded personalities.

The Broken in Heart

He healeth the broken in heart. . . . He telleth
the number of the stars.   —Ps. 137:3, 4

A COLLEGE STUDENT of the freshman class came to talk with me about his religious ideas. He said: "I am not a member of any church and I have no creed. I don't believe in creeds."

"What, then, do you believe?" I asked.

"I believe that character is the most important thing in the world," he said.

I looked at the youth seated before me and said: "My friend, I congratulate you on your magnificent creed. Now, if you think about this a little more and ask yourself why character should be regarded as the greatest thing in the world, you will find that your conviction must be undergirded by a deeper faith; that the lives of all of us are determined by our creed, by the totality of our outlook on the universe."

In Psalm 147 two remarkable affirmations are made concerning God. "He healeth the broken in heart. He telleth the number of the stars." The first deals with his relationship to man; the second with his government of the universe.

For our purpose today we shall reverse the Psalmist's order and deal with the second affirmation first: "He telleth the number of the stars." These Hebrew words may be translated: "He fixes [or determines] the number of the stars."

It is an awesome experience to contemplate the divine

126

creative activity. A little more than ten years ago I stood one evening in the observatory on Mt. Wilson, California. The well-known astronomer, Dr. Ellerman, was my host. He had given forty years of his life to a study of the heavens. I said to him: "It certainly must require a massive intellect to grasp the pattern of creation."

The scientist answered: "On the contrary, the Creator's methods are remarkably simple. At the same time, of course, they are exceedingly profound. Such concepts as relativity and the quantum theory are highly complicated, but many of the laws that operate throughout the universe are readily understandable to the mind of man."

I said: "Will you please explain that?"

The astronomer continued: "For instance, we know that there are ninety-two chemical elements in the universe. Everything we see around us is fashioned of some or all of these ninety-two elements." Then pointing to a table he said: "You see that spectroscope there? By means of it we have positively identified fifty-eight of these elements in the fires of the sun. We are confident that the other thirty-four elements are there, although they may be present in such small quantities that we cannot apprehend them." Glancing at a printed chart he said: "Among the chemicals most abundant in the sun are calcium, iron, hydrogen, sodium, nickel, cobalt. Every sun, every star, every planet, every meteorite in the universe is made of some or all of these ninety-two elements. This is the basic material which the Creator used in fashioning the cosmos."

"May I trouble you with one more question?" I asked the astronomer. "Have you ever tried to visualize how that creative process occurred?"

"Why, yes, I have not only tried to visualize it; I have seen it in operation," he said.

When I looked rather astonished, he added: "With this great telescope I have explored time and again the giant nebula in the constellation of Orion; as I study that vast, rolling spiral of matter so immense that it dwarfs our entire solar system, I feel as though I am looking into God's workshop, and watching him as he fashions new solar systems."

As we stood talking there on the summit of Mt. Wilson, darkness began to descend on us. Far below, we could see the twinkling lights of Pasadena and Los Angeles. Above us the stars came stepping out one by one, marshaling their hosts and taking their appointed places in the canopy of heaven. As we watched this unforgettable panorama I understood why Tycho Brahe, the Danish astronomer, always put on his court garments before entering the magnificent observatory given to him by the king of Denmark. As he himself remarked, he was about to enter the audience-chamber of the Creator of the universe.

Now, I am fully aware that there are those who challenge this avowal of faith and some who emphatically deny it. The skeptical response has been made on numerous occasions, but never more eloquently than by Bertrand Russell, who has been aptly described as "a lonely survivor of the bitterest of Victorian agnostics." There is one thing that must be said for Bertrand Russell. He has courageously faced the full implications of his skepticism. That is more than can be said for many people who toy with agnosticism today. Professor Russell took his sad lantern and wandered with it down all the corridors of human thought, carrying to its logical conclusion his denial of God. He sets forth his conclusions in flawless English:

Man is the product of causes which have no prevision of the ends they are achieving, that his origin, his growth, his hopes and fears, his loves and beliefs are but the outcome of an accidental collocation of atoms . . . that all the labor of the ages, all the devotion, all the inspiration, all the noonday brightness of human genius, are destined to extinction in the vast death of the solar system, and that the whole temple of Man's achievement must inevitably be buried beneath the debris of a universe in ruins.

Now, that is magnificent prose, but a bleak and despairing philosophy. He declares that the whole universe originated by chance and that man, a by-product, was flung off by a blind, materialistic cosmos, and that everything in the end will be overwhelmed in universal ruin and death.

If the masses of people all around the world accepted this as their creed, then the will to live would perish in the hearts of men, and death would become the normal pursuit of the human race.

From this depressing view we return to the inspiring affirmation of the psalmist: "He telleth the number of the stars." It is worthy of note that the leaders of scientific thought in our time have, on numerous occasions, proclaimed the falsity of the doctrines of fortuity or chance. Kirtley Mather, of Harvard University, writes: "We live in a universe not of chance or of caprice, but of law and order. Its administration is completely rational and worthy of the utmost respect. . . . The administration has certainly not been functioning in a blindly mechanical manner. Instead it has proceeded in much the same way as would an intelligent, persevering and purposeful person. . . . One gets a definite sense of sympathetic relationship between oneself and the infinite creative power. . . . You have faith that spirit with spirit can meet." So the clearest thinkers of our day join with the psalmist in his avowal spoken centuries ago: "He telleth the number of the stars."

Yet if we stop there, with an affirmation only of the creative intelligence and power of God, the human heart will remain unsatisfied. Man looks out upon this incredibly vast universe, and, aware of his own physical insignificance in contrast with these immensities, longs for something more than a great Engineering Intelligence that brought these worlds into being. He wants to be sure that the universe is friendly; he grows lonely contemplating the stars.

Man hungers for the assurance that he is not alone in this limitless universe, and that behind these shining points of light is a love that embraces all things. He craves the divine companionship.

Have you ever noticed the opening words of the Apostles' Creed "I believe in God the Father Almighty"? So often when we recite the Creed we fail to notice that word "Father." God is not merely creative Intelligence; he is our Father in heaven. That was the very essence of the revelation of Jesus. He taught us that this is the Father's world, the Father who

> Stills the raven's clamorous nest
> And decks the lily fair in flowery pride.

He marks the flight of the sparrow; watches over his human children with compassionate solicitude; numbers the hairs of our head; loves each one in his vast human family as though he had but one child to love.

Human love at times reveals something of the quality of the Love divine. It is generally agreed that one of the best-loved chaplains in the Canadian forces in World War I was Colonel Scott, Chief of Chaplains. Always Chaplain Scott was to be found where danger lurked and his men needed him. Some years before the war he wrote this beautiful poem:

> I rose at midnight and beheld the sky
> Sown thick with stars like grains of golden sand,
> Which God had scattered loosely from his hand
> Upon the floorways of his house on high.
> And straight I pictured to my spirit's eye
> The giant worlds, their course by wisdom planned,
> The weary waste, the gulfs no sight hath spanned
> And endless time forever passing by.
> Then filled with wonder and a secret dread
> I crept to where my child lay fast asleep
> With chubby arms beneath his golden head.

What cared I then for all the stars above?
One little face shut out the boundless deep,
One little heart revealed the heart of love.[1]

Now tell me where that love originated? Did it come
from "an accidental collocation of atoms" in a cold, blind,
mechanical universe, or is love born in the hearts of men
because first of all it existed in the heart of him who created
us in his own image? Not only does he fix the number of
the stars, but also "he healeth the broken in heart."

"Yes," somebody says, "that is lovely poetry, but there
may come a day when that little curly head is snatched away
from its pillow and nothing is left but precious memories
and a breaking heart." That is true; that may indeed happen.

It happened to the man who wrote that poem! The little
son, grown into manhood, enlisted in the Canadian Army,
and served in France. While his father, in another section
of the battlefront, was valiantly caring for the spiritual
needs of his men, word reached him that his boy had been
killed in action, and was buried in an unmarked grave.

In his autobiography Chaplain Scott tells us of the night
he journeyed to a battlefield freshly plowed with shrapnel,
and, guided by a soldier who had fought over this ground
with his boy, sought to locate his resting place. With enemy
shells passing constantly overhead and only the fitful light
of the moon to illumine their way, they searched the rain-
drenched, broken earth for signs of a new-made grave. At
last they found it. Tenderly they bore him away to a military cemetery, where the Chaplain himself conducted the
burial service. As he read the glorious and triumphant words:
"I am the resurrection and the life, saith the Lord, he that
believeth in me, though he were dead, yet shall he live . . ."
there came to him suddenly the sense of a divine companionship comforting and upholding him—the companion-

[1] "The Heaven of Love." Used by permission.

ship of a Father who had also given a Son. In the hour of his Gethsemane Chaplain Scott learned the meaning of the psalmist's words: "He healeth the broken in heart."

Life has not been easy for many of you. The road has been rough and steep. Bitter disappointment, disabling illness in hospital or home, heartbreaking bereavement, or just the heavy sense of life's futility has dogged your footsteps. To you I bring not the philosophy of an accidental, purposeless, mechanical world in which man lives out his little day before vanishing into nothingness, but rather the Good News of our God, who is too great to be lost amid his stars, and who speaks to his human children in the midst of their tragedy and pain, saying: "O heart I made, a heart beats here."

He is our Friend, the unseen Companion of our journeying, our unfailing Ally on many a hard-fought field, the Home of our souls. He is the heavenly Father revealed by Jesus Christ, the Father who "telleth the number of the stars," who "healeth the broken in heart."

The Triumph of Immortality

*And with great power gave the apostles witness
of the resurrection of the Lord Jesus: and great
grace was upon them all.* —ACTS 4:33

ONE DAY in ancient Rome a noble-looking man whose princely toga marked him out as a patrician made his way to
Necropolis, the City of the Dead. Picking up a funeral lamp,
he lighted it and watched its flickering flame, a fitting symbol
of the transitoriness of our life on earth.

He set the lamp down at a tomb on which was engraved
but one word, "Tullia." Bowing down before the tomb,
Cicero cried: "Oh, my daughter, is this the quenching of
thy life?" This plaintive cry from the Roman Necropolis
echoed that of broken hearts all around the world who
"hopeless, laid their dead away."

Not far from the tomb of Tullia stood a monument dedi-
cated "To the Eternal Sleep." The Latin inscription ran as
follows:

> I was not and I became;
> I was and am no more.
> So much is true, all else is false,
> Traveler, drink, play, come.

Pitirim A. Sorokin, of Harvard, publishing the results of
his research into the literature of ancient Rome, Greece,
and Egypt, says that with the decay of belief in God and
immortality these civilizations degenerated into a riot of
bestial cruelty, and an unrestrained search for sensual pleas-

133

ures. Wealth and luxury, too, were flaunted to an extent
probably never equaled in any century of recorded history.
One incident alone will suffice to illustrate what I mean.
Cleopatra, queen of Egypt, in the course of one of the ex-
travagant banquets she gave in honor of Mark Antony,
thrilled her guests by exhibiting a lustrous pearl, flawless and
wonderful to behold. It was passed around from guest to
guest for their admiration. The pearl was valued at what
in our time would be three-quarters of a million dollars.
When the jewel was handed back to her, she dropped it into
a glass of vinegar, and when the pearl was dissolved, drank
the liquid.

This blatant extravagance was manifested side by side
with unspeakable poverty and wretchedness. Sixty million
slaves crowded the Empire. In some sections of it the slaves
were so numerous that they were forbidden to wear the
badge of their servitude lest they should become aware of
their numbers and turn upon their masters. Their lives for
the most part were at the whim of their owners. In one instance four hundred Roman slaves were executed because
one of their number had murdered his master.

This was the world into which Christ came. "It had burned
itself out in sin, had rotted down its ideals through luxury
and self-indulgence, through skepticism and cynical indifference. Into that world of doubts and fears, of shame and
decay, of sensuality and senile despair, Christ built Calvary,
and from the hour that he hung on the cross there was
hope."

It would seem on that black day amid the blasphemy and
torture, the nakedness and death of Golgotha that all the
evil of the world made its supreme challenge to the
sovereignty of God. When the disciples saw their Master
die, it looked to them as if their cause was finally lost. John
Masefield, in his play *The Trail of Jesus*, makes Longinus,
the Roman centurion, say to Pilate's wife: "He was a fine
young fellow, my lady, not past the middle age, and he was

all alone and defied all the Jews and all the Romans, and when we had done with him, he was a poor broken-down thing dead on the cross."

This was apparently the universal verdict—"a poor, broken-down thing dead on the cross." But that conclusion omitted the one most important factor in the drama on Calvary—it left out God. The triumph of evil was only a seeming victory, for on the third day God revealed his power in the Resurrection of Christ.

The personal transformation of the disciples is the most convincing evidence of this transforming power released in the world on the first Easter Day. These men, so helpless and empty-hearted, so broken in spirit on the day of the Crucifixion, became recreated individuals. Hesitancy, cowardice, and fear were swept away. They moved and lived with confidence in a new world. Their Master was really alive. He had triumphed over all the forces of evil. He had mastered death and the grave. Appearing suddenly in their midst as they were meeting together, he said to his disciples: "Peace be unto you," and then commissioned them to go forth and win the world for his kingdom. Thus ordinary, commonplace men, were transformed into spiritual giants who swept across the Roman Empire proclaiming the gospel of their crucified but risen Lord. Right to the heart of the Empire in Rome they went, so that Paul in a later letter to the Romans could ask to be remembered "to the saints that are in Caesar's household." They penetrated even into the palace of the brutal Nero: "And with great power gave the Apostles witness of the resurrection of the Lord Jesus." Their testimony was irrefutable, and they sealed it with their blood. Every one of the Apostles, with the exception of John, is believed to have been martyred. They rejoiced that they were counted worthy to die for the Master whom they loved and served.

One of the notable converts to Christianity before the close of the second century A.D. was Tertullian, an able scholar. Immediately he became one of the most powerful advocates of the new faith. He wrote: "Go on you, good governors; the mob will think you all the better if you sacrifice Christians to them; crucify, torture, condemn, destroy us; your injustice is the proof of our innocence. . . . The more you mow us down, the greater our numbers become; our blood is the seed from which new Christians spring."

In the Roman arena they were torn to bits by famished lions and their bodies, smeared with oil and tar, were set ablaze to light up the festivities in the emperor's garden. Men, women, and little children went unflinchingly to their undeserved doom.

How pale, anemic, and selfish does our modern profession of Christianity appear in contrast to these heroic and devoted believers of the early centuries! As of old the voice of Christ is challenging us today: "Whosoever would come after me, let him deny himself, and take up his cross and follow me."

This was the faith of two Christian missionaries, Mr. and Mrs. Lee of Calcutta, India. They sent their six little children to a school in Darjeeling, situated in the hill country. Then one terrible night of storm, the monsoon rains came down in torrents. The hillside on which the little cottage was situated was swept away by the onrushing waters, burying the six children amid its ruins. One little lad lived long enough to tell the story of what had happened on that awful night. He said that the oldest sister had called the rest around her, telling them: "You mustn't be afraid. We are in God's hands. Remember what Daddy used to tell us," and then he added, "We were all kneeling in prayer when the hillside slipped away, and we were buried."

This tragedy seemed to the parents so purposeless that their hearts were utterly broken, but when the first wave of desolating grief had subsided, they said: "Our little family is gone, so we must establish now a greater family of neglected little ones." They went out into the streets of Calcutta gathering up the abandoned children of India, and made a home for them. For more than thirty years they cared for three hundred little ones annually, and were like a father and mother to them all. When at last they raised a memorial to their own six children who had perished on the hillside, what do you suppose was the inscription they placed on it? These words: "Thanks be to God who giveth us the victory through our Lord Jesus Christ."

There is only one effective rival to Christianity in the world today, and that is the philosophy of Marxism. Both of these beliefs challenge the allegiance of all men. The goal of each is universal supremacy. They are unalterably opposed to each other. One sets forth the Easter faith in the power of God and in the inherent dignity and eternal worth of man; the other espouses a militant atheism, affirming that man is no more than an economic animal. It is not by accident that human freedom prevails most where the Christian gospel is proclaimed, for it affirms that man as a child of God possesses inalienable rights which no state is entitled to take away.

The Marxist philosophy regarding man is expressed in the pessimism of Ecclesiastes: "Man's fate is a beast's fate; one fate befalls them both; as the one dies, so dies the other; man is no better than a beast."

In contrast Christianity affirms to those whose trust is stayed on God: "Beloved, now are we the sons of God, and it doth not yet appear what we shall be! but we know that, when he shall appear, we shall be like him; for we shall see him as he is." Wherever the Easter faith has taken root in human hearts, a new dignity and worth is given to human life. It creates steadfast personalities who stand like a rock in the face of every wind of adversity that blows. They are a shelter to less resolute lives.

In our lifetime humanity will make a choice between these two world views. Either Christianity or Marxism will be

practically universal. To which of these philosophies will
the world give its allegiance? Which way will the balances
fall? On whose banners will victory rest?

Let it never be forgotten that the most powerful factor
in the world today is the influence of ideas. They are more
powerful than warships and planes and guns. Ultimately
they will win the world, one way or another. Either the
triumph of godlessness and the supremacy of one class in
human society or the universal brotherhood of all men under
the overarching fatherhood of God—these are the conflicting
ideologies of our time. Each of us may well ask: "What am
I doing that victory may come to the cause of Christ and
his kingdom?" Is your loyalty a once-a-year loyalty? Is
your devotion one that bows its head for a brief moment
at the Cross of Christ, and then goes its indifferent way careless of the fate of mankind? If so, then you are a part of the
world problem rather than a factor in its solution. If so,
the thorn-crowned Christ cannot count on you.

A fresh baptism of spiritual power swept over the ancient
world on the first Easter Day and won it for Christ, that is
a repeatable miracle. A little more than ten years ago I was
in Russia, before the present measure of religious freedom
was granted. It was the policy of the Society of the godless
to give atheistic lectures, especially on the days set apart for
religious festivals. One of our party told us of a dramatic incident that happened a few years earlier. A militant atheist
was addressing a large audience of Russian people on an
Easter evening. He poured ridicule and scorn upon the
Christian doctrine of the Resurrection. When the lecturer
concluded his address, he asked if there were any questions.
A young priest at the back of the hall indicated that he would
like to say a few words. He walked to the front, but neither
asked questions nor offered any argument. He faced the
audience and repeated the greeting which for centuries
Russians have given to each other on Easter morning, saying:

"Christ is risen!" As one man the audience arose and answered him with a familiar response: "Verily, he is risen!"

God speed the day when as the Easter greeting is uttered "Christ is risen!" the peoples of every nation in the whole round earth will rise up as one man and reply: "Verily, he is risen!"

THE CHALLENGE OF RESPONSIBILITY

What Are You Living For?

For to me to live is Christ.   —PHIL. 1:21

A WELL-KNOWN Presbyterian minister on the West Coast was invited to address a group of college students in their fraternity house. At the commencement of the meeting he turned to the chairman and asked: "What are you living for?" The student replied: "I am going to be a pharmacist."

The minister said: "I understand that this is how you are going to earn your livelihood, but what are you living for?" The youth bowed his head for a moment, and, then, looking up with clear, true eyes, he said: "Sir, I am sorry, but I haven't thought that thing through." It was discovered that of the thirty students present only two had asked themselves this question. They all knew how they would earn their livelihood, but only two had discovered the central purpose of life.

We should keep clearly in mind the distinction between our livelihood and what we are living for. Jesus had a livelihood. He was a carpenter by trade, but that was not what he was living for. Andrew, Peter, James, and John had a livelihood. They were fishermen, but that was not what they were living for. Paul was a tentmaker, but that was not what he was living for.

How would these followers of Christ have answered the question asked of the young American student? How would Paul have answered it? Without an instant's hesitation he would have flashed back the answer: "For me to live is Christ. That is what I am living for."

This brave old Christian warrior began to reckon his life from the day when Christ laid his hand upon him on the road to Damascus. Straight through the center of Paul's life ran a line of demarcation. It has been suggested that he had his own calendar—on one side of which was B.C., before he met Christ, on the other side, A.D., the year that followed his call to apostleship. On the one side was the old life with its tension and inner conflicts; its slavish keeping of the law. On the other side was the new man, the new life, and the encompassing love of Christ.

For Paul this line of demarcation went down to the very roots of his being. There had been a revolutionary inward transformation. He expressed it like this: "When any man comes to be in Christ, there is a new creation. What is old is gone—the new has come."

Dante Gabriel Rossetti oftentimes pondered the miracle of spiritual rebirth. He made frequent sketches with pencil, oil, and water colors, trying to depict the wonder of it. Finally, the concept that was growing in his mind flowered forth in a pen-and-ink drawing entilted: "The Conversion of Mary Magdalene." The scene is laid in the street outside the house of Simon, the Pharisee. Mary, bedecked with flowers and accompanied by her lover and their boon companions, is passing down the street in careless pleasure. Suddenly through the open door she catches sight of the Master's face, and their eyes meet. The tender, searching eyes of Jesus penetrate beyond the woman that she is to the woman that she might yet become. In that instant her soul awakes.

The artist concentrates on two individuals: One is Mary Magdalene, with her profound contrition, and her proud resolve to enter into the new life she sees opening before her; the other is Christ, with an unforgettable look of tenderness and sorrow, of entreaty and redeeming love. Oblivious of the efforts of her companions to stop her and of the jeers of some of them, Mary begins to climb the steps to the open door of Simon's house. She sees only one face, the face of her Redeemer, and, leaving all, she goes to follow him.

Something of the same experience is described by John Masefield, the British poet, in *The Everlasting Mercy.* These are the words of Saul Kane, the drunkard and wastrel:

> The bolted door had broken in.
> I knew that I had done with sin;
> I knew that Christ had given me birth
> To brother all the souls on earth;
> And every bird and every beast
> Should share the crumbs broke at the feast.[1]

Whenever I have a few spare moments in Boston, I always go to Trinity Church to look into the strong, yet tender face of Phillips Brooks, the spiritual giant whose likeness has been preserved for us by a renowned sculptor. He stands at a pulpit with the open Bible before him, and behind him stands Jesus, his hand on Brooks's shoulder.

I have often wondered how Saint-Gaudens was inspired to create this noble work. Certainly it presents the truth regarding Phillips Brooks.

In his memoirs is an intimate and revealing letter which he had written to a dear friend. It reads: "All experience comes to be but more and more the pressure of Christ's life upon ours. I cannot tell how personal this grows to me. He is here. He knows me and I know Him. It is no figure of speech; it is the realest thing in the world." Why should we wonder that the man who wrote these words made people feel, as they came into his presence, that they were very close to the Master? He, too, could say with Paul: "For me to live is Christ." The whole aim and influence of his life was Christ. His master passion was to bring men and women who knew not Christ to the place where they could behold

[1] Copyright 1911 by John Masefield. Used by permission of the Macmillan Co., publishers.

him in his strength and kingliness. That is what he was living for.

Here is the only effective answer to human needs. Here is the one true hope of man. There are those who tell us that the hope for peace in the future can best be secured by teaching the nations to fear war by making them realize that man possesses today destructive forces so powerful that they can wipe out vast cities and even nations; that the only alternative to human suffering on a scale never before seen in the history of the world is to maintain peace on earth.

Fear is a powerful force and does exercise a restraining influence. However, I do not believe that fear alone can bring peace to the nations. It is true that all the governments of the world and all their peoples prefer peace to war. It is equally true that all of them want some things that are not compatible with peace. They want the right to exploit the natural resources of peoples far beyond their borders. They yearn for national aggrandizement. They cling to the right of a militant assertion of national sovereignty in every possible situation, and many of them seek to impose their will upon other nations.

There is a dream of peace in the hearts of multitudes around the world today, but there is also a dream of power. Despite the restraining influence of fear, if ambitious men see an opportunity to grasp power, they will gamble the world's safety to reach their goal. Fear is rampant throughout the world, but it is not sufficiently constructive to unite the nations; rather, it tends always to divide them. Fear cannot create one world united in brotherhood and peace. Love only is capable of this colossal achievement.

On the world's horizon there is but one Personality great enough to transcend all divisions of nationality, race, and clime—the One who came to reveal the divine Fatherhood of God and the universal brotherhood of man. But that Fatherhood and that brotherhood exist for us only potentially until within our hearts is enshrined his love and until in our lives his spirit is expressed.

The average citizen of the United States has very little conception of the enormity of the problem facing the world today. More than half the population of the earth is living among scenes of ruin and desolation. Rev. J. Hutchison Cockburn, Director of the Department of Reconstruction and Church Aid of the World Council of Churches, at Geneva, came to this country from Europe and gave us an eyewitness account of the desperate situation there. He quoted the estimate made by a civil engineer of the labor that would be involved in clearing Berlin of the vast accumulation of rubble. The engineer said that it would take fifty trains each with fifty trucks, working every day for seventeen years, to transport the rubble and refuse out of the environs of Berlin. He had recently stood in the center of Warsaw, and found it impossible to tell where the streets had formerly run. In the vast heaps of debris, millions of rats were living, and the foxes had come in from the open country to feed upon the rats. To those of us who saw Warsaw only a few years before the beginning of World War II, this picture would be utterly incredible were it not given to us by a reliable witness.

But that is not the greatest problem. In a few decades the ruined buildings can be restored. The real problem is shattered human lives, utterly disillusioned and bereft of hope. Not only must a stupendous task of material construction be performed, but an even greater task of spiritual restoration, particularly among the youth of Europe, who during the time of the Nazi occupation were taught to lie, to cheat, to sabotage, to steal, and even to kill. They must now be re-educated and given moral and spiritual ideals.

There was never a time in the history of the world when the truths that Christ taught and the kind of life that he lived were more desperately needed by the world. All who believe in his way of life and who seek to follow him must dedicate themselves with renewed consecration to the enterprises of his kingdom. Christians, it is true, are in a minority in most of the countries of the world, but minorities have been used of God more frequently than majorities, in bringing about tremendous spiritual advances. The influence of Christian personalities is out of all proportion to their number. In China, for instance, before the war only one person in every six thousand was a Christian, but in China's Who's Who every sixth name is the name of a Christian.

When Paul wrote, "For me to live is Christ," he meant us to understand that Christ was the master passion of his life, because he believed with all his heart and soul that Christ and Christ alone had the answer for the world's needs. Wherever he looked in past or present, within or without, above or beneath, everywhere he saw only Christ. He saw the power of Christ changing the world of the Roman Empire in which he lived, making men and women kindlier, more forgiving, more patient, more noble, more clean, more compassionate, more loving. Christian love was to him the greatest force in the world. For us, too, it is the only power that can heal the wounds of the world.

Mankind has been sickened with an orgy of hate that has rent the world asunder, and left in its wake millions of broken hearts. Only love can bind up these wounds. When I speak of love, I am not thinking of that emotion of which the crooners sing and which is represented so frequently in the modern movies and novels. The word "love" has been largely spoiled by some of the modern interpretations of it. It is not a sickly, sentimental, selfish thing; it is clean, virile, compelling. That which is called love today, even in a romantic sense, is oftentimes not love at all; it is lust.

Shakespeare, with his incisive mind, differentiates between the two:

Love comforteth like sunshine after rain,
But Lust's effect is tempest after sun;

Love's gentle spring doth always fresh remain,
Lust's winter comes ere summer half be done;
Love surfeits not, Lust like a glutton dies;
Love is all truth, Lust full of forged lies.

The love of which Paul speaks is a Godlike love that shines forth in all its fullness in the life of Jesus Christ. Paul has written an Ode to Love. It is to be found in First Corinthians, thirteenth chapter:

Love is very patient, very kind;
Love knows no jealousy;
Love makes no parade,
Gives itself no airs, is never rude,
Never selfish, never irritated,
Never resentful;
Love is never glad when others go wrong,
Love is gladdened by goodness, always slow to expose,
Always eager to believe the best,
Always hopeful, always patient.[2]

Henry Drummond says that he knew a man who read this chapter once a week for three months, and it changed his life.

If we would read it every day in the morning, read it thoughtfully and prayerfully, it would change the tenor of the entire day, and before long would transform each one of us. If we incorporate the spirit of these words into our lives, everything we do will take on eternal value. This is what we Christians are living for.

[2] I Cor. 13:4-7 from *The Bible: A New Translation* by James Moffatt. Copyright 1935 by Harper & Bros.

Making Your Life Significant

Take therefore the talent from him, and give it
unto him which hath ten talents. —Matt. 25:28

THE WORDS of judgment and condemnation in our text were spoken by a lord to his servant. The latter is described as "wicked and slothful." He has failed in an important trust. The thing which he neglected has been taken from him.

It is a mistake to think that this is simply an arbitrary sentence on the part of a judge. What Jesus has enunciated is a natural and spiritual law which is universally true. Employ a capacity and it will grow and expand. Neglect it and it will wither and die. That is natural. It is inevitable.

We see the operation of this law in the realm of biology. Primitive forms of sea life illustrate it. Far below the surface of the ocean is darkness, and silence, and deadly cold. But in these almost unfathomable depths there is life—life that is sustained by microscopic food raining down from higher levels. In these mysterious regions of the deep, life exists precariously. One of two things happens to the eyesight of the fish. Either it begins to deteriorate and disappear or else it enlarges and expands. Down in that abyss there are fish with headlights like automobiles. Others have lights along their sides that make them look for all the world like an ocean liner at night. Some of them have experienced a development of the eye to such an extent that it catches the faintest ray of light and has enlarged to two-thirds of the size of the creature's head.

150

On the other hand there are fish whose eyes have deteriorated. They have been brought to the surface and when examined they seem to have normal eyesight. But one incision of the scalpel and a glance with the lens reveals that behind that seemingly perfect eye there is a mass of ruin. The optic nerve is "a shrunken, atrophied, insensate thread." Eyes have they but they see not for their vision has perished. They had developed other faculties, but they ceased to use their eyes and the inevitable penalty followed. Nature said, "Take the talent from them." The disuse of function is always followed by the decay and loss of the faculty.

This principle is equally true whether we think of the brain of a scholar, the hand of a musician or the voice of an operatic star. These gifts of God—these talents entrusted to us—must be employed or else they will decay and disappear.

Even more graphically this law is demonstrated in the spiritual realm. The faculty that distinguishes man from all the rest of the animal kingdom is his capacity for spiritual expression. In his body there are a hundred resemblances to the higher animals, and in some of the nobler creatures there is even the rudiment of reason. But man is possessed of a faculty that lifts him to a plane far above all created things for in his soul is "a vast capacity for God."

If this heavenly gift is employed, man advances in Godlikeness and in strength and beauty of character. If it remains unused and neglected, his spiritual nature shrinks and shrivels and contracts until every trace of the Divine has disappeared. So Tennyson asks:

> For what are men better than sheep or goats
> That nourish a blind life within the brain,
> If knowing God, they lift not hands of prayer . . . ?

If every Godward aspiration of the soul has been allowed to become extinct, and every inlet that was open to heaven to be choked, and every talent for religious love and trust to be persistently neglected and ignored what remains except decay and death? Like the thunders of judgment we hear the proclamation of this eternal law—"Take the talent from him."

It is significant that in Jesus' parable it is the man with only one talent who neglects it. Great ability is subject to great temptation. The highly endowed individual will either direct his powers nobly or else he will misdirect them disastrously. But at least he is not tempted to bury his talents. It is the many—those who belong to the rank and file of life —who need to ponder this parable.

"I have no ability," you hear somebody say. Have you ever said it? "I have little to offer the world. What can I do?" Feeling that they cannot play a conspicuous part in life, they retire altogether from the stage. They take the talent that God has entrusted to them and looking at it pityingly they say, "Is that all?" Then they wrap it carefully in a napkin and bury it in the ground.

Shakespeare in "Measure for Measure" says:

> Heaven doth with us as we with torches do,
> Not light them for themselves; for if our virtues
> Did not go forth of us, 'twere all alike
> As if we had them not.

The man or woman who has one talent and proceeds to bury it, typically illustrates for us what the psychologists call "an inferiority complex." This is how it is defined: "A group of ideas, the central one of which is disbelief in oneself, in one's values to the community, and in one's abilities in this or that direction, with a strong charge or feeling of helplessness and fear."

Now turn back to Jesus' parable: "Then he which had received the one talent came and said, . . . I was afraid, and went and hid thy talent in the earth. Hasn't that a modern sound? Fear of difficulties; fear of people, especially strangers; fear of criticism; fear of standing up to life—all these are the earmarks of inferiority.

Well, what is Christ's remedy for this sickness of the human spirit? He possesses the power of making us believe in ourselves and in the talent entrusted to us. He teaches us that God has planted within each of us a specific endowment that has been granted to nobody else. There are no two people in the world with the same fingerprints, and even more truly there are no two people in the world with the same endowment of mind and heart and body. We must set about discovering, exploring, and then employing the resources that God has given us—our resources of personality. There is no one to whom God has not entrusted a precious gift. And there is no one of us who is employing that gift to the full.

> No man is born into the world whose work
> Is not born with him; there is always work
> And tools to work withal, for those who will.

Lowell might have added that unless we employ the talent entrusted to us, this special contribution which God intends us to make can never be made.

When you say therefore, "I have no ability, I have nothing to offer the world," you are not merely reflecting on yourself—you are reflecting on God. So Edwin Markham sings:

> To each man is given a day and his work for the day;
> And once, and no more, he is given to travel this way.
> . . . .
> There is waiting a work where only his hands can avail;
> And so, if he falters, a chord in the music will fail.[1]

The lack of faith in one's mission in life is the cause of multitudes of failures. When you have learned to believe in God's purpose for you as an individual, you are immediately

[1] Used by permission of Virgil Markham.

lifted out of the mass and become significant and meaningful
in the eyes of God and of man.

But you say, "I have only one talent. So many people are
better equipped than I. I must leave the world's work to
them." Do you know that God is unceasingly using one-
talent people to accomplish his purposes?

After reading the inscription on the monument to the
memory of Lord Shaftesbury, I thought of all that this
great man had done for the social life of Britain—of his battles
fought on behalf of little children whose tender lives were
blighted by the twelve- and sometimes sixteen-hour day
down in the coal mines; of the prison reforms he accom-
plished; of his labors on behalf of the Ragged Schools for
Boys; of the laws enacted on behalf of the chimney sweeps
and other exploited classes.

On the day his funeral service was held in Westminster
Abbey, it seemed as if the whole of England had emptied itself into London. Tens of thousands of people—working men
rubbing shoulders with nobility—stood in the rain and thousands of them wept. He went down to his grave amid the
benedictions of the poor.

"There was a ten-talent man," you say. "How he inspires
us!" But Lord Shaftesbury would never have become "the
Great Emancipator" if his heart had not been fired with the
love of God. And who was responsible for that? Not his
mother, not his father—because they thought of nothing but
empty, vain, social activities. It was a servant in the home by
the name of Maria Millis who taught him how to read the
Bible and how to pray, and who stamped the character of
Christ upon the mind and heart of a little lad. Lord Shaftesbury carried to the day of his death a gold watch she gave
him with her blessing.

A ten-talent man—yes—but never could he have performed his remarkable tasks if Maria Millis, a one-talent
woman, had not been faithful to the call of Christ. And there
came a day when that self-effacing, humble soul stood in the

presence of her Master, and heard him say: "Well done, thou good and faithful servant: enter thou into the joy of thy lord." Lord Shaftesbury himself did not hear greater commendation than that.

One day in the last century another young lad sat in the gallery of the British House of Commons and listened to the majestic eloquence of John Bright. He went back home with the resolve in his heart that he was going to be a lawyer. The day before he was to sign the articles in a law office, he was walking through his native city when he came face to face with his Sunday-school teacher. He said: "I am signing the articles in a law office tomorrow." The Sunday-school teacher said, "That is a great profession," and then his face clouded and he continued, "but Henry, I have always hoped that you would be a minister of Christ." In deep thought, the youth went to his home and there in solitude he heard the call of the Eternal ringing in the chambers of his soul "as clearly as the morning bell rings in the valleys of Switzerland" and John Henry Jowett entered the Christian ministry. In Great Britain, and in America he exercised a ministry second to none in the twentieth century.

Yes, a ten-talent man, but if that one-talent Sunday-school teacher had failed in his responsibility, the Christian Church would have lost a consecrated minister.

I think of the day when that humble Sunday-school teacher stood in the presence of his Master and in glad surprise heard him say: "Well done, thou good and faithful servant: enter thou into the joy of thy lord." And John Henry Jowett didn't hear any greater praise when he stood in the presence of the King of kings.

"I have no ability. I have nothing to offer the world."

Never say that! Take that gift that God has entrusted to you, no matter how humble it may seem to be, and use it in the service of Christ and your fellow men. He will make it glow and shine like the very stars of heaven. And you will learn to believe in yourself and in your mission in life, because you have learned to believe in him.

Nowhere else is there greater opportunity for the exercise of your talents than in the Church of Jesus Christ, where there is work for all.

Let us resolve to take the gift that God has entrusted to us, and to use it from this day forward in the service of his Kingdom. Then at last when our little day draws to its close, when the sands of time have almost run out and the shadows are lengthening from the West, when earth and earthly things are drifting from our sight and we stand before him in that day to which there is no sunset and no dawn, may we hear him say in a voice sweeter than the strains of celestial harmony: "Well done, good and faithful servant; thou hast been faithful over a few things, I will make thee ruler over many things: enter thou into the joy of thy lord."

You Are the Hope of the World

*If the foundations be destroyed, what can the
righteous do?*
—Ps. 11:3

A PROMINENT LEADER in Washington said recently that man
must obtain "a sufficient mastery of nature so that permanent
world peace will be a reality and not a mere hopeful expression of faith."

That observation, it seems to me, misses the central issue.
Many of our most baffling problems today are due to the fact
that man has achieved a mastery of nature, a mastery that
now threatens to reduce our civilization to "a vast, slightly
radioactive wilderness, devoid of human life."

What man needs is not a greater mastery of nature, but a
mastery of himself, and of those destructive tendencies that
are separating the nations into hostile warring camps.

"If the foundations be destroyed, what can the righteous
do?"

Well, the foundations are being destroyed before our
eyes today. The civilization that this generation has known
is passing into eclipse, and the shape of the new one has not
yet emerged.

In the last five years a succession of world-shaking events
have transpired. Here are a few of them:

Germany disappeared as a great nation.

Japan ceased to exist as a world power.

China began to awaken to her opportunity for world
power.

The atomic age was ushered in.

157

Russia emerged from centuries of eclipse to become a first-class world power.

The United Nations Organization came into being.

Any one of these six events might well be regarded as an epoch in the course of a hundred years, yet all of them have happened in half a decade.

The most important development of all I have not mentioned with these six: The common man all around the world is awakening to a realization of his right to freedom and self-determination. Revolutionary propaganda is accelerating the process.

We are so close to present-day events that the average man or woman has little understanding of the events happening before our eyes. Like Rip Van Winkle, we are sleeping through a revolution.

Have you noticed what is happening in China, in Burma, in the Dutch East Indies, in the Philippines, in India, in South America, in Egypt, in Palestine, in French Morocco, and even in such conservative nations as Italy and France?

The entire world is in ferment today. We are living in a changing age. There is a seething unrest among the masses especially in colonial countries. They are demanding the right to self-rule everywhere, and the privilege of developing their own national resources.

Dr. Soong, President Executive of China's Nationalist Government, said recently: "Asia is tired of being regarded only in terms of markets and concessions or as a source of rubber, tin, and oil, or as furnishing human chattels to work the raw materials."

You can feel the intensity behind these words. There is revolt in every corner of the world against the supremacy of the white race.

During the second half of the eighteenth century the world witnessed two great revolutions: the American, and, later, the French, but the total effect of these two upheavals combined would be insignificant in comparison with the revolution that is happening at this time.

Now, there are some people who will tell you that it is just a temporary unrest, and if expedients are applied here and there, it will all end in placidity and peace.

Did you ever hear of Dame Partington? She was referred to in the British House of Commons by George Canning, one-time Prime Minister.

Dame Partington lived in Sidmouth, England, in 1824. There was a great flood that year. It was so great that it swept over a considerable part of England. The Atlantic Ocean rolled into Sidmouth, coming right to the doors of the people.

In the midst of this sublime and terrible storm, Dame Partington was seen on the doorstep of her house on the beach. She had a pail and a mop. She dipped her mop into the sea water flooding her home and wrung it out on her doorstep. Said Mr. Canning: "The Atlantic Ocean was aroused, and the spirits of Dame Partington were up, but it is needless to say that the contest was rather unequal. The Atlantic Ocean won."

It is as futile to suggest that any temporary alleviative will stem these vast movements toward human freedom as it was for Dame Partington to tackle the Atlantic Ocean single-handed with her mop.

Revolutionary forces, too, are advancing. For instance, take the two conservative nations to which I have referred—Italy and France. In Italy 4,300,000 Communist votes were polled. In France more than 6,000,000 Communist votes were polled. In Italy, the Communist party has signed up more than two million members. Partially, of course, this is a revolt against the Roman Catholic Church. Even more, it is a desperate attempt on the part of hungry masses of human beings to find some measure of economic security.

"If the foundations be destroyed, what can the righteous do?"

Well, ancient and venerable foundations are cracking and

sagging before our eyes. Familiar landmarks are disappearing; buoys in the channels of history are being swept from their moorings and carried away. Not merely the maps of the world are being changed; the face of the world is being altered, and the end is not yet in sight.

"If the foundations be destroyed, what can the righteous do?"

What are the people who believe in God to do? What prophetic word has Christianity to utter in this time of crisis?

Some people are saying: "Let the church retire within herself and forget the outside world. Let her develop a kind of pietism, and concentrate on individual religion."

Well, that is exactly what happened in Germany. That is the reason why the Nazis were able to paganize the nation and prepare for a global war. The church retired within itself and said: "The affairs of the world don't concern us."

One of the main reasons Martin Niemöller spent eight years in a concentration camp was because he was one of the few German Christian leaders with vision enough to realize what was happening in the nation. He read and interpreted the handwriting on the wall.

A similar policy of retirement within itself has been adopted by the Orthodox Church in Russia. That is the only reason why the Soviet government permits it to continue.

A totalitarian regime tolerates only that which is of some use to it, and the Orthodox Church is now of use to the Russian government. So its members are allowed to say their prayers, to sing hymns in the church, and to kneel in corporate worship. But no word must be spoken in criticism of government policies within the nation or outside it. The church must remain silent, even though its leaders believe that the policy of their government is an imminent threat to the peace of the world. There you have a perfect illustration of the perils of individual religion that is blind to larger issues.

What I am pleading for is an intelligent Christian approach to national and international problems. It is important that

Christians be informed on what is happening in the world, and that they resist every attempt to make the Church a mere tool or mouthpiece of the State.

"If the foundations be destroyed, what can the righteous do?"

What can Christians do?

Well, if they have faith in God and are zealous for the kingdom of Christ, they may take heart, because they will see that the period in which we now live is remarkably similar to the day in which Christ came with his gospel of the Kingdom of God.

In the years preceding the downfall of the Roman Empire there was the same seething unrest, the same upthrust of the masses, the same cry of spiritual desolation.

It was a despairing world into which Jesus came two thousand years ago. It "had rotted down its ideals through luxury and self-indulgence, arrogance and avarice. Doubts, skepticism, and despair were on every hand. It was a world of shame and decay, of sensuality and senile despair."

Into this world, so dark and hopeless, came Christ with his gospel of love and of brotherhood and of self-sacrifice. From the hour that he hung upon the cross and rose triumphant from the dead, hope was born in human hearts.

The Apostles of Christ set forth into every corner of the decadent Roman Empire with the good news of God's Kingdom, calling on all men to repent that they might become the children of that Kingdom.

The Christian gospel goes far beyond Marxism in meeting the needs of the world. It declares that there must be a reformation of individual character before we are fit to be citizens of God's Kingdom.

Experience has amply demonstrated that an order that is based only on economics and politics will create its own tensions and frictions. No matter how noble may be the Utopia that we erect, the human stuff of which it is composed will bring about its destruction.

When once this personal reformation has been effected, and we have learned to live as brothers in God's world, the Christian gospel expects us to become crusaders against the evils that still remain. The gospel of Christ has a message for the individual, and one also for society.

The man whose life has been touched by the spirit of Christ will begin at once to let that spirit affect him in all his social relationships.

Someone has pointed out that the two most searching questions in the opening chapters of the Book of Genesis are these:

First: "Adam, where art thou?"

Second: "Where is thy brother?"

The Church of Jesus Christ must insistently ask these two questions: "Where are you? What are you doing with your life? What is your relationship to Christ?" Secondly, "Where is your brother? What is happening to him?"

If we answer the first question and disregard the second, we are not true Christians. We have not embraced the Christianity of Jesus Christ. The fact that no real progress has been made by the United Nations Organization in the matter of world peace is not the fault of the Organization. The trouble lies within the hearts of those who make up its membership. It lacks a spiritual foundation. It is like the house of which Jesus spoke that was built upon the shifting sand.

The only enduring foundation for a Temple of Peace is good will, a recognition of the rights of others, a readiness to understand their viewpoint, and a willingness to sacrifice one's own interests for the common good of all.

The problem of establishing a new world order is basically a spiritual one. It may well be that in the full perspective of history the stalemating of our present efforts may prove an ultimate blessing. It may cause the leadership of the nations to recognize that the fundamental issues are not economic and political, but moral and spiritual.

"If the foundations be destroyed, what can the righteous do?"

No foundation is ever destroyed unless there is rottenness in it, and there has been plenty of rottenness in twentieth-century civilization: plenty of injustice, ill-will, greed, hate, and selfishness. God is shaking the whole world today; he is shaking our Western civilization, and I believe that the awakening of the oppressed races is but part of the divine plan for his earthly children.

It is a painful business to live through this period of stress, change, and revolution, but the foundations of God's Kingdom are not shaken. His purposes cannot be frustrated or defeated.

In the midst of the present turmoil the Christian may well look up and lift up his head, knowing that his redemption draweth nigh.

What can the Christian do in such a time as this? He can pledge himself with renewed loyalty to the Church of Jesus Christ as it witnesses to his gospel in this and other lands.

There is nothing hesitant or apologetic about the crusade of Communists in our high schools and colleges, our labor unions and factories. They believe that the triumph of one class in society is the answer to the world problem. Do we believe that Christ has given us a better answer than the economic or political? If we believe that, let us say so unashamedly and courageously. We must not let any group of men on earth outstrip us in the proclamation of our convictions.

The early Christians were ready at any moment to die for their faith. Are we ready to live for ours? This will require something more than attendance at church one day a week. It must enter into every aspect of our life. We must out-live and out-think those who would destroy our heritage. As we

witness fearlessly for Christ, lifting high his Cross, and tread-
ing where his feet have trod, he will draw all men unto him.

Soldiers of Christ, arise,
    And put your armor on,
Strong in the strength which God supplies,
    Through His eternal Son.

To Hear and to Do

*For there is no difference between the Jew and
the Greek; for the same Lord over all is rich unto
all that call upon him. For whosoever shall call
upon the name of the Lord shall be saved. How then
shall they call upon him in whom they have not believed? and how shall they believe in him of whom
they have not heard? and how shall they hear without a preacher? and how shall they preach, except
they be sent?* —ROM. 10:12-15

GAMALIEL BRADFORD, the American biographer, in his *Life
of Dwight L. Moody* makes the assertion: "The sermon has
been the great blight upon the Protestant church." That
statement is convincing evidence of the fact that even a brilliant man may totally misjudge a situation. The truth is that
the sermon was one of the most powerful factors in produc-
ing the Protestant Reformation, and through all the centuries
since it has helped to maintain "the liberty wherewith Christ
has made us free."

Ruskin in the "Stones of Venice" declares that the Reformation was a "re-animation," a rediscovery of truths long
obscured. He calls it "The re-animated Faith, and in its right
hand the Book open."

Far from being a "blight" the sermon is of the very genius
of Protestantism.

John Bunyan pictures for us the Puritan preacher in unforgettable phrases: "His eyes were on heaven, . . . the best of
books was in his hand. The law of truth was written upon his

lips. The world was behind his back. He stood as if he pleaded with men."

There is no other function of the Christian Church that draws us so close to the ministry of our Lord as preaching the Word. When the people of Capernaum sought to detain Jesus in their own city, he said: "I must preach the Kingdom of God in other cities also, for therefor am I sent." The last commission that he gave to his disciples before his ascension was spoken in these words: "Go ye into all the world and preach the gospel to every creature."

Paul, in his letter to the Romans, tells of the rich mercy of God unto all men: "whosoever shall call upon the name of the Lord shall be saved." Then he pauses to ask: "But how then shall they call upon him in whom they have not believed? and how shall they believe in him of whom they have not heard? and how shall they hear without a preacher? and how shall they preach except they be sent?"

Frequently that last sentence is taken to mean that we should send forth missionaries who will preach the Word, but the reference is not to man at all; it is to God. It is God who calls, who equips, and who sends his messengers forth. The spiritual giants of every century have been aware of this. So we hear Joseph Parker saying: "The ministry of Christ is not a profession. Ministers of the right kind are called from eternity, and they cannot help uttering what is in them, and they are not always aware of the reach of their own meaning." Then he adds: "If any young men are coming into the ministry as a profession, God hinder them; build up a great granite wall right in the face of them, and starve them until they begin to repent and pray."

That was the conception of preaching in the minds and hearts of all the great prophets of Israel. So we have Jeremiah shrinking back from the challenge, pleading his inadequacy, his youth, his inexperience, but the divine compulsion is laid upon him. "If I say I will not make mention of him or speak any more in his name, then there is in my heart as it were a burning fire shut up in my bones, and I am weary of forbearing, and I cannot contain."

He must speak forth the message that God has laid upon his heart. So it is with all the prophets: Moses in the lonely wilderness, standing before a burning bush and hearing a voice that says: "Take off thy shoes from off thy feet, for the place whereon thou standest is holy ground." Then follows the summons to go with God's message on his lips to an ungrateful and rebellious people.

Isaiah saw the Lord high and lifted up, and his glory filled the temple. Isaiah cried: "Woe is me; I am undone! I am a man of unclean lips, and I dwell amid a people of unclean lips, for I have seen the King of kings, the Lord of hosts." Then in a moment of utter self-surrender he prostrates himself before God and prays: "Here am I; send me!"

Ezekiel, under the spell of the divine Presence, bows himself to the ground, and hears the urgent command: "Son of man, stand upon thy feet and I will speak unto thee."

These men felt that the hand of God was laid on them. They could not do otherwise. The divine restraint drove them on.

Paul says:

"For though I preach the gospel, I have nothing to glory of. For necessity is laid upon me. Yea, woe is unto me if I preach not the gospel."

One of my deepest convictions is this: No man should take upon himself the vocation of the Christian ministry unless he believes beyond all peradventure that there is no other work on God's earth to which he dare turn his hand and his heart.

Does the present-day preacher feel that divine compulsion? Does the call of the Eternal ring in all the rooms of his soul? Does it summon him as it summoned Peter from his nets, and Matthew from the receipt of customs? If so, why do men call the sermon a "blight"? Why has the twentieth-century placed an interrogation mark over against the Christian pulpit? Why do secular magazines and journals discuss questions like these: "Is the Pulpit Decadent?" "Has Preaching a Future?" "Is the Sermon Obsolescent?"

Laymen today undertake to tell us exactly what is required in a preacher. Here are some of the things they suggest: He must have a clear delivery, a good personality, a sound education and a thorough knowledge of the Bible, fluency of speech and acquaintance with life, and the ability to hold the attention of men and women.

When a pulpit is vacant in a great church in this nation, its officials send out to Chicago, or to Pittsburgh, or to Kansas City, or to Los Angeles—nay, they send to Britain, to Scotland, to Australia, to Wales, to Canada, to South Africa, seeking a man who will possess these characteristics. Yet I declare to you that a man can have every one of these characteristics, important as they are, and yet not be a great preacher. Strange that we should forget the one supreme qualification without which the voice of the man in the pulpit, no matter how eloquent it may be, will become "as sounding brass and clanging cymbals." What is this qualification? As he opens the Bible and brings its truth to bear upon the hearts of the men and women in the pews they will hear the sound of another voice echoing in and through the preacher's words—a voice that is searching, probing, judging; a voice that comes from they know not where, but deep within their souls they feel that it is the voice of God. That is the *sine quo non* of preaching, and no theological seminary can confer it upon a man, and no endowment of eloquence can replace it.

How shall they preach except they be sent of God, and a live coal from the altar of the Eternal be laid upon their lips? Then, all the native gifts, and all the discipline of years of study and preparation will become the vehicle of God's message from the heart of a personality fired with the conviction of a divine mission.

Every time that God has had a word to speak to a generation, he has not lacked a man to utter it. When the corruption of the Christian Church in the sixteenth century cried out unto God for judgment, He raised up the mighty reformers. There would have been no Reformation in Germany without Luther; there would have been none in Switzerland without Calvin; there would have been none in Scotland without Knox; there would have been no Evangelistic Revival in Britain without Wesley, and there would have been none in America without Jonathan Edwards and Dwight L. Moody.

When John Wesley preached to the multitudes, at one time to the country folk, and at another to the miners who came up from the pits and listened until the tears streaming from their eyes made little rivulets through the grime of their faces, what was the thing that brought his message to bear so powerfully on their hearts? Let one of them tell us. John Nelson writes:

As soon as he got upon the stand, he stroked back his hair and turned his face upon me where I stood. He fixed such an awful dread upon me even before he began to speak that it made my heart beat like the pendulum of a clock. When he did speak, I thought that all his whole discourse was aimed at me. . . . I durst not look up, for I imagined all the eyes of the multitude were looking at me.

In the voice of John Wesley, Mr. Nelson heard another voice—the accents of the Eternal God speaking to his soul and drawing him to that fountain which is open for sin and uncleanness. It is this note of divine authority which alone makes preaching effective.

When Louis XIV of France heard Massillon preach, he remarked: "I have heard several great orators preach and have been much pleased with them; as for every time I hear you, I am much displeased with myself."

Finally, the message which God lays upon the heart of

his messenger cannot accomplish its full mission without the co-operation of the hearers.

It is a remarkable fact that while hundreds of books have been written on the subject of preaching and thousands of lectures have been delivered on the same theme, so far as I know no book or lecture has been written on the important subject of listening. If the sermon does not grip us or interest us, we usually blame the man who stands in the pulpit. He is "dull" or "uninteresting" or "prosy."

Jesus never sanctioned such an attitude. He laid the responsibility squarely upon those who hear God's Word. Of course, the message ought to be presented arrestingly and with power, but the final responsibility for the hearing of that word rests on the one who listens.

"Every one who heareth these sayings of mine and doeth them shall be likened unto a wise man who built his house upon a rock."

"He that hath ears to hear, let him hear."

"If any man heareth my voice and openeth the door, I will come in to him."

"Take heed how ye hear."

"Blessed are your ears, for they hear."

Great hearers make great preachers. A congregation that is spiritually alive, eager, sympathetic, receptive, will develop preaching power in a man who has any gift whatsoever. The best preparation for the worship of God is made when the worshiper approaches the sanctuary, saying reverently to himself: "What will God's message be for me this morning?"

Adequate preparation for hearing the Word of God is not easily made when our minds are filled with worries, cares, distractions, business anxieties, personal antagonisms, misgivings regarding our health or the illness of a loved one, grief for someone we have lost. All these emotions are stirring within us as we approach the house of God. At times it seems as though life has presented us with problems that we cannot solve.

The poem "Tam I' the Kirk" reminds us that even romantic love may erect barriers to effective worship.

He canna sing for the sang that his ain he'rt raises,
He canna see for the mist that's afore his een,
And a voice drouns the hale o' the psalms and the
  paraphrases,
Cryin' "Jean, Jean, Jean!"

Many people come into the house of God with longings, aspirations, and feelings of desperate loneliness.

Others, again, enter church in the same mood with which they go to a moving-picture house—not a word of prayer, not a single entreaty to God that he will speak to their souls, and no effort to arouse disciplined attention.

One man said to me recently: "The entire service became transformed for me when on a Sunday morning I suddenly realized that every part of the service was an act of worship."

A few years ago, with a group of friends, I journeyed by rail from Geneva to Chamonix, in France. I recall looking out of the train window. The foothills were shrouded in mist, and the landscape presented a rather dreary appearance. We were depressed. Suddenly, as the train rounded a wide curve, the clouds lifted and the sun broke through. There, towering before our eyes in solitary majesty, lifted almost fifteen thousand feet above the level of the sea, stood Mont Blanc, its white dome shining in the sunlight clothed with a million tons of virgin snow, lifting its crest to heaven like a great thought held up to God. All sense of disappointment and weariness left us, and we were filled with spiritual exaltation and a deep and abiding peace.

So, too, week by week men and women gather in the house of God. Some of them are tense and restless. Some are discouraged and depressed. Some are unable to see for the multitude of their tears. Some are crushed by the weight of life's burdens. Some are lonely and frustrated. All of them need God. If they have come together in the spirit of expectant faith, somewhere in the service they hear a Voice from the world of the Eternal, and in one radiant moment the vision of God breaks upon their souls.

So are they cleansed, empowered, ennobled, lifted out of defeat and failure into the victory that overcometh the world.

The Holy Catholic Church

By this shall all men know that ye are my disciples, if ye have love one to another.—JOHN 13:35

A NEW YORK businessman said to me recently: "I attended a service of worship in your church a few weeks ago. When the congregation stood and recited the Apostles' Creed, I was greatly surprised, especially when they repeated the words 'I believe in the holy catholic Church.'"

I explained to the man that the Apostles' Creed was one of the creeds in use by all Christians before the final break between the Eastern Orthodox Church and the Western or Roman branch, and that most Protestant churches accept the creeds of the undivided Church.

"But," he said, "what about that phrase, the 'holy catholic Church'? Do you believe in that, too?"

"Yes, we do," I replied, "you see, the word 'catholic' is derived from the Latin *catholicus*, which means 'general' or 'universal.' So when we affirm, 'I believe in the holy catholic Church,' we are saying, 'I believe in the universal Church composed of all who truly follow Jesus Christ.'"

The earliest use of the word "catholic" as applied to the Christian Church is found in the writings of Ignatius in the early part of the second century A.D. He writes in part: "Wherever the Bishop shall appear, there let the people be; even as where Jesus may be, there is the Catholic Church."

Jesus himself has taught us that he is universally present wherever his followers meet to worship him. In the second century the concept of the Catholic Church as the church

173

universal "where Jesus may be" was still maintained. After that date, with the gradual departure from New Testament Christianity, the growth of the hierarchical conception is increasingly manifested up to the time of the Protestant Reformation. As Dean Inge has observed: "After the second century, the apologists for the priesthood are in smooth waters."

The word "catholic" is clearly defined in the Scotch Confession of Faith of 1560. Referring to the holy catholic Church it says:

"Which kirk is catholic, that is universal, because it contains the elect of all ages, all realms, all nations, all tongues . . . who have communion with God the Father and with his son, Jesus Christ."

It would be difficult to find a better definition than this. Whenever, therefore, we say "I believe in the holy catholic Church," an innumerable host of Christians rise up before us in spiritual vision—the vast invisible congregation of Christians whose names are known only to God. That is the "holy catholic Church."

For many years, and especially after the Protestant Reformation in the sixteenth century, the Western or Roman branch of Christianity claimed exclusive rights to the title "Holy Catholic Church."

In a catechism which is on sale in most Roman Catholic churches this question is asked: "In which church are these attributes of the Holy Catholic Church found?" The answer is: "These attributes of the Holy Catholic Church are found in the Holy Roman Catholic Church alone." When the adjective "Roman" is introduced, the original definition of the word is lost; thus, one branch of Christianity arrogates to itself as its sole prerogative that which belongs properly to all true Christians.

This exclusive claim is even more expressly made in a pamphlet entitled "Freedom of Worship—The Catholic Position." Its author is Francis J. Connell, and it is published by the Paulist Press. It carries the imprimatur of Francis J. Spellman, archbishop of New York, now cardinal. I quote:

They [the Roman Catholics] believe that the Catholic Church is the only organization authorized by God to teach religious truth and to conduct public religious worship. Consequently, they hold that any creed which differs from that of the Catholic Church is erroneous, and that any religious organization which is separated from the Catholic Church lacks the approval and authorization of God. . . .
From this it follows that, as far as God's law is concerned, no one has a real right to accept any religion save the Catholic religion, or to be a member of any church save the Catholic Church, or to practice any form of divine worship save that commanded or sanctioned by the Catholic Church. . . .
Such then is the first Catholic principle relevant to religious liberty—that man has not an unqualified right to practice any religion he may choose. . . .
Neither does it necessarily oblige others to allow him the unrestricted practice of his religious beliefs. [Italics mine.]

Up to this point the enlightened Protestant will smile and go his way worshiping God according to the dictates of his conscience and enjoying the privilege of religious freedom. The italicized sentence at the close of the above quotation, however, may leave him with a vague feeling of uneasiness. He may begin to suspect that the ever-advancing claims of Rome might yet imperil his liberty.

When a religious organization makes the explicit and unequivocal claim to be the sole custodian of the truth and the sole dispenser of the grace and salvation of Almighty God, it is only a short step from that claim to a militant denial of the right of any other church to teach or propagate its faith. This has now happened.

Here is a book, *Catholic Principles of Politics,* written by Father John A. Ryan and Professor Francis J. Boland of Notre Dame University. It bears the imprimatur of Archbishop Spellman, now cardinal. On page 318 we read:

The fact that the individual may in good faith think that his false religion is true gives no more right to propagate it than ... the perverted ethical notions of the dealer in obscene literature confer upon him a right to corrupt the morals of a community. . . . Now the action of preaching and writing are at once capable of becoming quite as injurious to the community as any other actions and quite as subject to rational restraint.

Now, there are two fallacies in this paragraph which should be obvious to all, The first is the suggestion that the Protestant religion is false. This is simply a biased judgment passed by one branch of Christianity upon another, carrying with it no moral or spiritual authority so far as we are concerned.

The second is the suggestion that Protestant writing and preaching may be as injurious to the public as obscene literature. This assertion is demonstrably false, since Protestant preaching and teaching has produced in this nation tens of thousands of the noblest men and women in American history. "By their fruits ye shall know them."

It was this Protestant teaching and preaching which also laid firm and strong the moral and spiritual foundations of the American nation.

According to Justin Wroe Nixon, out of four million inhabitants in the American colonies in 1763 there were only about twenty-two thousand Roman Catholics. As G. P. Gooch, the noted historian, has said: "The democratic church has grown into a democratic State." And that democratic church was Protestant to the core.

Protestants are not unduly disturbed even when Roman Catholic leaders publish detractions of our faith. We begin to be alerted and alarmed, however, when they declare their right to limit Protestant religious freedom if and when they should become a majority in the nation.

In *Catholic Principles of Politics* (pages 320 and 321) it is frankly stated as an "eternal and unchangeable truth" of the Roman Catholic Church that whenever that church secures a position of overwhelming majority in a nation, it has the right to expect the state to impose restrictions on all non-Catholics in their religious teachings and propaganda, and to deny them privileges extended to the Roman Catholic Church, such as exemption from taxation. Then we are assured that while this is all true "in logic and theory," American Protestants need not be alarmed since such a dominant position cannot be gained by the Roman Catholic Church for years to come.

These comforting words fail to reassure us, however, when we see what is happening under our eyes in various Roman Catholic countries around the world. A Roman Catholic priest in Brooklyn sent me a clipping from *The Tablet*, one of the publications of his church, containing an article on non-Catholic minorities in Spain. It denied categorically that there is any persecution or repression of Protestants in Spain. Protestants are allowed to distribute their literature and their churches are open, and are distinguished by large visible signs to indicate that they are Protestant places of worship.

In the summer of 1948 I determined to go to Spain and investigate the situation at first hand. In talking with more than a score of Protestant ministers and visiting as many churches, I discovered that all Protestant schools in Spain, once housing seven thousand pupils, are closed and the children required to go to schools where Roman Catholic instruction is compulsory. Protestants are not permitted publicly to bury their dead with the rites of their churches; to print hymnbooks or Bibles; to reply in the public press to any attacks made on them; or to place any signs on their churches denoting they are places of worship. They have been jailed and fined for holding meetings of Bible study and prayer in their homes. There have been repeated disorders, culminating in the case at Linares on June 27, 1948, with attacks on Protestant worshipers by thirty Catholic youths using rubber truncheons and brass knuckles.

The Spanish constitution of June 17, 1945 (Section six), reads: "The profession and practice of the Catholic religion, which is the religion of the Spanish state, will enjoy official protection. No one will be molested for his religious beliefs nor for private adherence to his code. No public ceremonies or manifestations will be permitted in any religion other than the Catholic religion."

In the summer of 1948, Cardinal Pla y Deniel, primate of Spain, on behalf of all Spanish bishops and archbishops stated that any interpretation of this section which indicates that it permits public worship on the port of Protestants is a perversion of the law, which permits only private worship by Protestants in Spain.

On September 10 of last year Cardinal Segura, bishop of Seville, issued a pastoral letter denouncing the Protestants and demanding abolition of "these centers of false religions in Spain." A few weeks later the first of a series of attacks on Protestant churches began, and the Catholic Action Youth left leaflets amid the wreckage of the pews declaring, "The Holy Inquisition did not limit itself to talking. We make ourselves heirs of the Inquisitorial Spirit."

One of the Protestant pastors makes this rather pathetic appeal: "We hope that public opinion in free countries will make Catholics ashamed of what the Catholic Church is doing in Spain, and that they will oblige the pope and the Spanish prelates to be reasonable concerning us as you are with the Catholics living in the Protestant countries."

In ordinary times such proceedings would be deplorable. Today, when anti-Christian forces in the world threaten to blot out all religious freedom, it is tragic and unthinkable that any one branch of the Christian faith should seek to deny to others the right to witness for the gospel of their Lord and Master, whether they are a minority or majority in any nation. This is of the very essence of religious freedom and democracy as we Americans understand it.

If there were only one thousand Roman Catholics in this

nation, our American concept of religious freedom would afford to them the fullest expression of their faith, both in public worship and in religious propaganda.

Let it not be forgotten that one of our four freedoms for which our sons fought and bled and for which many of them died was freedom of religion. It is utterly absurd for any branch of Christianity to claim that it has a monopoly of truth or virtue or of the grace of God, especially when we have the opportunity day by day of brushing shoulders with its adherents.

Dean Inge of London made a typically incisive comment at this point: "It is becoming impossible for those who mix at all with their fellow men to believe that the grace of God is distributed denominationally."

In November, 1947, the Rev. Father Ford, a tolerant, courageous, public-spirited Roman Catholic priest, delivered an address in Boston in which he pleaded for Protestant and Roman Catholic churchmen to meet around a conference table and settle their differences.

Approximately a year earlier Bishop G. Bromley Oxnam called upon Cardinal Spellman and made a similar proposal to him. Nothing has yet come of these suggestions, and it is very doubtful if anything will.

A recent address by Archbishop Cushing of Boston would seem to have closed the door on any hope of such a friendly conference.

How should we react, as Protestant people, to this situation? Our text has the answer: "By this shall all men know that ye are my disciples, if ye have love one to another."

There is no place in Christianity for intolerance and hate. It is unchristian and un-Christlike. "A new commandment I give unto you," said Jesus: "That ye love one another; as I have loved you."

Our Lord clearly understood that this world can never achieve the brotherhood of man until Christian brotherhood has been demonstrated within the ranks of the Church of Christ.

By what right can Roman Catholic and Protestant leaders exhort the nations of the world to compose their differences when their own controversy remains unresolved? We call upon the Jews and the Arabs to show mutual tolerance, when Christian minorities in many nations are hindered in the exercise of their faith simply because they are minorities. How may we expect rival ideologies to exist side by side in peace throughout the world if different interpretations of Christianity cannot live side by side in peace within the bounds of this nation?

Let us continue to cherish in our hearts love and good will for those who differ from us. This is the hallmark of genuine discipleship. At the same time, we must continue to be alert to every threat which endangers the religious freedom which is our birthright. If we lack Christian love in our hearts, no profession of creedal loyalty to Christian dogma will ever qualify us as true disciples of our Lord.

As we look back over the history of this nation what a thrill of pride sweeps over us as we see the notable roles that Protestantism has played in our history! It laid the foundations of religious freedom whereby every man has the inalienable right and privilege to seek for truth and to worship God according to the dictates of his conscience, none daring to make him afraid. It has contributed richly to the rise of American democracy, wherein the form of government is determined by the governed, and their rulers are responsible to the people. It put the Bible into the hands of the common people, making them familiar with the Scriptures, which teach from Genesis to Revelation that the individual stands in immediate relationship to God, and that divine grace and salvation are available without any human intermediary.

Let us never forget, however, that every privilege brings a corresponding responsibility. May we hold ever aloft the torch of truth passed on to us by the hands of our fathers, so that its kindling rays shall penetrate to earth's remotest boundaries, carrying into lands where intolerance and darkness and slavery reign the light and the love and the liberty of his gospel who said: "By this shall all men know that ye are my disciples, if ye have love one to another."

One in Hope and Doctrine

Is Christ divided?   —I COR. 1:13

A YOUNG MAN walked into my study with a troubled look on his face and laid a book down upon my desk. He said: "I am greatly disturbed by some questions regarding our Protestant religion. This book says 'The spirit of internal discord and dissension has split Protestantism into so many hundreds of warring sects.' What is your answer to this contention?" he asked. That youth is not alone in his perplexity. When the World Council of Churches met in Amsterdam, the delegates from many European and Asiatic countries were bewildered to discover that there are more than two hundred divisions of Protestantism in the United States. This situation has no parallel in any other country on earth. In European countries one finds one or two or at most five separate branches of Protestant Christianity. Why should this strange and confused situation exist in the United States?

A very great service was rendered at the meeting of the World Council of Churches by Dr. Samuel M. Cavert, General Secretary of the Federal Council of Churches of Christ in America. With directness, clarity, and simplicity he explained to the delegates the reasons for the unusual religious situations existing in this land. The first is this: This nation is composed of a cross section of all the peoples of the world. In simple truth, it is a "melting pot" of peoples and races. In particular, all European races and nationalities are represented here. They imported with them the religious differences existing in the countries of Europe. They were accus-

182

tomed to worship in their own language in their homeland, and they continued the practice in the United States.

Soon European national churches began to appear in the nation from the Atlantic to the Pacific. Take the Lutheran Church, for instance. It has twenty separate divisions. When it was founded here there was a Swedish Lutheran Church; a Danish Lutheran Church; a Finnish Lutheran Church; a Norwegian Lutheran Church; a German Lutheran Church; an American Lutheran Church, and so on. But now that the use of European languages is gradually being discarded for a uniform English service, the way is prepared for the amalgamation of all these national branches of the Lutheran Church. Even now practically all divisions of the Lutheran Church are united in the National Lutheran Council, so there is little purpose in the continuation of the divisions. In Philadelphia, recently, one of the leaders of American Lutheranism appealed to his church for an immediate union of all Lutheran bodies into one great Lutheran Church of five million members. Similarly, many of the divisions that appear today in Protestant churches in this nation are due to obscure controversies that occurred centuries ago in Europe.

In the second place, these divisions are not quite as alarming as some people would have us believe. Two hundred of them, if grouped together, would aggregate no more than 6 per cent of the total church membership of the nation. Many of them are made up of only a few thousand adherents. Furthermore, 80 per cent of all Protestants in the United States are grouped into eight denominational families: The Episcopalian, the Lutheran, the Presbyterian and Reformed, the Baptist, the Disciples, the Evangelical United Brethren, the Congregationalists, and the Methodists. Within another ten years denominational Protestantism will be greatly altered in the United States, since one of the most significant results stemming from the World Council of Churches is a progressive movement for amalgamation within these different Protestant groups.

Still another factor and a very important one is generally left unmentioned in discussions of this issue. The reason why these national churches were formed in the United States, as well as a large number of small denominational groups is, to the credit of this nation, due to the fact that there exists in America complete religious freedom.

In many countries of Europe—indeed, in most of them— there is an established church. American delegates to the World Council of Churches were astounded to discover how many European governments support established churches. These churches possess special privileges and prerogatives, and oftentimes political pressure is exerted on other Christians to induce them to join the State churches. In all too many instances they are persecuted if they refuse to conform.

The significance of the First Amendment to the American Constitution forbidding an establishment of religion is that all ecclesiastical bodies in this nation, large or small, receive equal treatment. There are no favorites of the State; all will stand or fall by their own strength or by their own weakness.

Now, in most countries of Europe, in sharp contrast to the American practice, churches are supported out of public funds. So behind the Iron Curtain we have the almost incredible situation of the salaries of thousands of clergymen, Roman Catholic and Protestant, being paid out of the funds of Communist regimes, because the churches are state-supported.

We possess in this nation the priceless privilege of religious liberty, the right of every man and woman in the nation to worship God according to the dictates of his own conscience. It is true that this privilege has actually increased the number of religious denominations, but we will neither surrender our freedom nor apologize for it.

We can have uniformity any time we wish. In many countries in Europe you will find few religious denominations, and those that are there exist perilously, because the deadening hand of religious and political oppression is laid upon them. Thank God this is not true of America, and we are not prepared to cast away our heritage. The separation of state and church in America every lover of freedom here will maintain and defend, for it is our most effective bulwark against the usurpation of the rights of the individual by the state. Mark these words: State absolutism can never exist in a nation where religion is free. We must keep religion free if we are to have political freedom.

You remember the old saying "He who pays the fiddler calls the tune," and European states from which the churches draw their support are now calling the tune. It is much easier for churches which are supported by the free-will offerings of the people to reject any and every attempt of the state to dominate the life of the church. So we will refuse to render to Caesar the things that belong to God.

What shall we say of the so-called "warring sects" of Protestantism? That is a fiction. Where in the United States is such "warfare" found? Protestantism is not made up of warring sects. The day of denominational theological controversies is past. It was demonstrated at the meeting of the World Council of Churches that Protestantism, world wide, has reached essential unity on all the basic doctrines of the Christian faith. We are "one in hope and doctrine," as we sing in the well-known hymn.

Now, with respect to denominational families, it is not true to say that you "will hear one gospel preached in the Episcopal Church, a different one in the Methodist, and another in the Presbyterian." Indeed, it is possible for one to go about from congregation to congregation and unless one reads the nameplate on the outside of the church, it is difficult to know with what denomination of Protestantism one is worshiping. That is why there is an increasing interchange of membership in Protestant churches, as people move from one locality to another.

Ministers, too, are constantly crossing denominational frontiers. Not only are there no warring Protestant denominations, but a profound sense of Protestant unity has been achieved. Not since the Reformation has this feeling of religious solidarity been so manifest in this nation and all around the world. A striking example of the freedom with which ministers cross denominational boundaries is seen in the Fifth Avenue Presbyterian Church, New York. Throughout a period of fourteen years Dr. John Henry Jowett, and later Dr. Henry Howard ministered to this church. Dr. Jowett was a Congregationalist, and Dr. Howard a Methodist. Both these ministers retained their denominational affiliations. During those fourteen years it was not felt by anyone that there was the slightest conflict or inadequacy in the preaching of these great men because they did not belong to the Presbyterian tradition. Let us forget this nonsense about an impassable barrier between our churches. It just doesn't exist.

In the forseeable future I do not believe that all religious denominations in this nation will be united into one great church. Indeed, it is highly questionable whether any such consummation is desirable. Christian common sense indicates that we must move forward in America to the amalgamation of individual denominations and to even larger unions as well. At the same time both the testimony of history and present experience warn against putting too much power into the hands of ecclesiastical officialdom, for by whatever name it calls itself it has resulted all too often in despotism and tyranny.

William Pitt said: "Unlimited power corrupts its possessor," and Lord Acton wrote: "Power tends to corrupt; absolute power corrupts absolutely." The history of the Christian Church, past and present, reinforces the truth of these words.

It is a noteworthy fact that divisions appeared in the infant Christian Church far back in ancient Corinth. Some of the people gathered around Paul. They called themselves the Pauline party. Another group gathered around Apollos, who reaped the harvest that Paul had sown—Apollos, the man of eloquence. Others gathered around Peter, and they called themselves the Petrine party. Then there were those who said, "We will have none of these; we belong to Christ."

Paul asked, "Is Christ divided?" Can he be parceled out in segments to various groups? Protestants all over this nation are asking the same question today.

Never was I more hopeful of the future of our faith in this nation and in the world. We are mustering our forces; we are closing our ranks; we are preparing for a great advance of God's kingdom. In these dark days, when every form of religion is under fire, the three great religious traditions of America—Jewish, Roman Catholic, and Protestant—should unite in defense of religious freedom, which is our strongest bulwark against civil oppression.

In the United States today, excluding children, there are forty-six million Protestants. If you add the children, there are more than fifty-two million in this country. Yet there is a vast resource of our Protestantism that is only partly utilized. This unemployed potential is the laymen. Look across the nation and you will see Protestant laymen leading in every department of life—in business, the professions, education, and politics. Tragically, however, they are not in the van of the Protestant Church. We have not yet succeeded in harnessing this magnificent potential.

We need the help of laymen to achieve church unity, for they can approach this issue with far fewer inhibitions than the clergy. We need their guidance in the highest church councils. We need the inspiration and encouragement of their Christian fellowship. In the good providence of God there is every indication that we shall witness this glad consummation. In every Protestant denomination there is a greater response on the part of laymen now than has been manifested in the past half century.

God is working his purposes out, and in humble dependence on his divine assistance, we pledge our loyalty anew to the faith of our fathers who laid firm and strong in religious freedom the foundations of our great Republic.

> He has sounded forth a trumpet
>   that shall never call retreat;
> He is sifting out the hearts of men
>   before His judgment seat;
> O be swift, my soul, to answer Him;
>   be jubilant, my feet!
> Our God is marching on!